All too often we think that the answer to (lives is to be given a dose of fresh techniques for praying – as though God were some kind of reluctant genie whom we have to conjure up by sorcery. The reason this book is such good medicine is that it gives us, not fresh techniques for praying, but a fresh vision of the God to whom we pray. In *Our Father* Richard Coekin paints a mouth-watering picture of what a joy it is to be able to turn to Almighty God and call him 'Father'. He walks us through the Lord's Prayer and shows us that it is bigger than the box we have sometimes put it in. The Lord's Prayer doesn't just give shape to our prayer life; it gives shape to the whole of our relationship with our Father in heaven. I think that is why I found reading this book such an inspiration to pray more. It reminded me that prayer is not just one of the things that Christians do, but that prayer is at the heart of how we live out the relationship with God that Christ has made possible.

Read *Our Father*, take in the Lord's Prayer and it won't just transform your prayer life, it will transform the whole of your Christian life. Having been so invigorated by *Our Father* myself, I can't wait to get everyone in our church reading it.
Mike Cain, Emmanuel Church, Bristol

Good theology that resonates with day-to-day life is a real treat. Reading *Our Father* will teach you some great truths about the God to whom we pray, but, even better, it will make those truths real to you on a Monday morning.
Tim Chester, author, speaker and church leader

Richard Coekin's exposition of the Lord's Prayer aims to move beyond mere understanding to enjoying God, as his subtitle attests. You can understand doctrine without enjoying God, but you can't enjoy God without first grasping sound biblical teaching. Once you get that, you must learn to use the doctrine in prayer. Richard's very clear, warm, and practical volume shows you how.
Tim Keller, Redeemer Presbyterian Church, New York City, USA

This is the kind of prayer classic we all ought to possess but not keep on a bookshelf. It needs to be read and referred to often; it is packed full of treasure.

Jennifer Rees Larcombe, author, speaker, and Director of Beauty from Ashes

This is a fantastic book, which will not only expand your understanding of how God wants us to pray, but will also make you want to do it. Read it and your prayer life could well be transformed.

Vaughan Roberts, Rector of St Ebbe's Church, Oxford

If you need help with prayer – read this book. It's sensational!

Al Stewart, Bishop of Wollongong, NSW

We know it by heart, but we don't know how to use it. Richard Coekin wonderfully awakens this sleeping giant of our prayer lives and puts flesh on the dry bones of our childhood repetition. I was just thrilled by this book, which gave me such a desire to pray a prayer that crystallizes Christ's priorities for our lives.

Rico Tice, Associate Minister, All Souls Church, Langham Place, London

Our Father

Our Father

Richard Coekin

Our Father

Enjoying God in prayer

ivp

INTER-VARSITY PRESS
Norton Street, Nottingham NG7 3HR, England
Email: ivp@ivpbooks.com
Website: www.ivpbooks.com

First published 2009
Reprinted 2009, 2010

British Library Cataloguing in Publication Data
A catalogue record for this book is available from the British Library.

ISBN 978–1–84474–393–3

Set in 11.5 / 14pt Dante
Typeset in Great Britain by CRB Associates, Potterhanworth, Lincolnshire
Printed and bound in Great Britain by Ashford Colour Press Ltd, Gosport,
Hampshire

Inter-Varsity Press publishes Christian books that are true to the Bible and that
communicate the gospel, develop discipleship and strengthen the church for its
mission in the world.

Inter-Varsity Press is closely linked with the Universities and Colleges Christian
Fellowship, a student movement connecting Christian Unions in universities and
colleges throughout Great Britain, and a member movement of the
International Fellowship of Evangelical Students. Website: www.uccf.org.uk

To my beloved Sian,
apart from the Saviour, God's greatest gift to me

How beautiful you are, my darling! Oh how beautiful!
. . . You have stolen my heart . . .
(Song of Songs 4)

and
the congregations of the Co-Mission Initiative

In all my prayers for all of you, I always pray with joy
because of your partnership in the gospel from the first day
until now, being confident of this, that he who began
a good work in you will carry it on to completion
until the day of Christ Jesus.
(Philippians 1)

Contents

Preface

When Jesus' disciples asked him for help with prayer, he gave them a beautifully simple but spiritually stunning outline known as 'the Lord's Prayer'. This extraordinary prayer has been cherished by Christians everywhere and always. In it, our Saviour has brilliantly summarized for us the kinds of request that God most delights to answer.

This book about the Lord's Prayer is called *Our Father* because, in his opening phrase, 'Our Father in heaven', Jesus spotlights the intimate relationship with God that motivates and shapes all prayer.

The subtitle of this book is 'Enjoying God in prayer'. Jesus knew that, when we struggle to pray, we need a fresh appreciation of God. More than techniques and rebukes, we need to explore his magnificent character and amazing plans. As we glimpse the Father described in Jesus' prayer, we find ourselves lifted in wonder to delight in him. Our cold hearts become warmed and our stifled tongues released to pray. The Lord's Prayer, and so this book, is all about enjoying God.

I am personally very excited about the Lord's Prayer. Being both sinful and an activist, I've never found the disciplines of prayer easy. But I do find the Lord's Prayer exhilarating. It has become a lifeline from God, constantly dragging my rebellious heart back to him. I couldn't survive without it now. As I've studied the biblical background to each phrase, I've discovered marvellous and sometimes terrifying things that propel us toward God. I'm convinced that these could be of immense help to Christians who struggle to pray. When our spirits boil up and our hearts cry out in frustration, 'Why *bother* – nothing happens when I pray!' the inspiration we need is supplied by Jesus in the Lord's Prayer.

Our Father is a fresh exposition of the Lord's Prayer for ordinary Christians. It's meant to be thoughtful, digging up the biblical background to Jesus' words, so that we better understand what he means. It's meant to be practical, with applied scenarios after each chapter, to help us think through various ways in which we might use the Lord's Prayer. Above all, it's meant to be about our Father, for, as we learn to enjoy him, we'll begin to enjoy praying to him.

I pray that this book may reveal something of the sparkling genius of the Lord's Prayer. May it renew in us the delights of praying to our Father, in the name of his Son, in the power of his Holy Spirit, in joyful confidence that this is a prayer he absolutely loves to answer. And to him be all glory for this dazzling gift.

Richard Coekin
January 2009

The Lord's Prayer

This, then, is how you should pray:

'Our Father in heaven,
hallowed be your name,
your kingdom come,
your will be done, on earth as it is in heaven.
Give us today our daily bread.
Forgive us our debts, as we also have forgiven our debtors.
And lead us not into temptation,
but deliver us from the evil one.'
(Matthew 6:9–13)

1 'This, then, is how you should pray . . .'

(Why we so urgently need the Lord's Prayer)

We all know that the quality of any relationship depends on communication. In our own lives, and throughout Christian history, the periods of closest communion with God are marked by an appetite for both hearing God's voice in Scripture and responding with passionate prayer. For Christians, prayer is like fresh air. Without it, we become laboured, sickly and weak, feeling cold and distant from our Lord. Indeed, it has rightly been said that 'Prayer is the highest activity of the human soul.'

The Bible everywhere rejoices, therefore, in the Christian privilege of prayer. It celebrates the God who hears our prayers: 'The eyes of the Lord are on the righteous and his ears are attentive to their cry.' It celebrates the peace we receive through prayer: 'Do not be anxious about anything, but in everything, by prayer and petition, with thanksgiving, present your requests to God. And the peace of God, which transcends all understanding, will guard your hearts and your minds in Christ Jesus.' It celebrates the blessings of answered prayer: 'You will receive whatever you ask for in prayer' (Psalm 34:15; Philippians 4:6; Matthew 21:22).

Given these great benefits of prayer, it is strange that Christians should so often be prayerless. As Joseph Scriven observed in his famous hymn of 1855:

What a friend we have in Jesus, All our sins and griefs to bear!
What a privilege to carry, everything to God in prayer.
O what peace we often forfeit, O what needless pain we bear –
All because we do not carry, everything to God in prayer!

So why don't we pray more?

Modern surveys reveal that evangelical Christians in the UK pray for an average of only five minutes a day. The figures for our leaders are not much higher. Church members often regard the congregational prayer meeting as the most unimportant and optional. Individuals feeling far from our Saviour commonly admit to chronic prayerlessness. Devotional prayer doesn't seem to be the engine driving many Western lives, ministries or churches. It is clearly very different in Chinese, African and South American churches, where prayer is a passion.

Why are we so prayerless in the West? We're familiar with the excuses: we're too busy, too stressed, too crushed by disappointment. We claim convenient scapegoats in partners or pastors who fail to inspire us to pray. But most of us recognize that we're infected with crippling secular attitudes.

We're riddled with *godless cynicism*, which renders us sceptical that prayer can make any real difference. So we rush around madly, desperately trying to change the world, but neglecting to talk to its governor in prayer.

We're addicted to *sensual apathy* that craves relaxing forms of entertainment. We can't bear to turn off the TV at night so as to be up in the morning to pray. So we wallow in worry, and neglect the sheer relief of passing our burdens to God in prayer.

We're sick from *selfish ambition* that cares little for God's priorities. We feel overwhelmed by busyness but continue to cram our diaries with a relentless search for relational fulfilment in both secular and church events, while neglecting the personal joy of time with our Father in prayer. We make time for Champion's League football or Facebook or fishing or the gym or chatting on the phone, but can't find time for prayer.

These attitudes make us chronically prayerless, and leave us feeling far from God.

It also has to be said that some Christians do live in circumstances that make prayer difficult. Disturbed nights with a screaming baby, long hours in a demanding job, intrusive flatmates or an unsupportive partner – all can make praying hard. But explaining our prayerlessness does nothing to reduce the spiritual sickness it creates.

We can't ignore the connection between poor prayer and a distant relationship with God. There are notable exceptions in most churches: the 'prayer warriors' whose commitment and ministry are a gift and an example for us all. But most of us remain permanently ashamed of our prayer life – there's very little 'life' about it. However impressive we seem in public, we know the sobering truth of those chilling words from Robert Murray M'Cheyne: 'What someone is alone on their knees before God, that they are – and no more.'

Prayer is both natural and unnatural to us

It is sometimes said that nothing is more natural for us than prayer. Certainly, we are created in the image of a relational God: Father, Son and Holy Spirit. In this sense, prayer is normal, 'wired into our DNA'. Indeed, almost everyone prays sometimes, whatever their religious outlook. A friend of mine from Belarus tells me that before he became a Christian, even as a committed atheistic communist soldier in Afghanistan, he nonetheless cried out to God for protection. The former Royal Navy chaplain Maurice Wood made a similar observation of the Second World War D-Day landings in France. There were suddenly no atheists among soldiers or crew, for everyone was praying! Prayer is natural for us because we're designed for it by our Creator.

Yet prayer is also profoundly *unnatural* for us, because of the dehumanizing corruption of sin. Outside Christ, all of us are spiritually dead to God. While those of many faiths will claim that prayer is beneficial as a form of meditation, they can know no personal communion with the living Lord and no answers to prayer. This is because our prayers as unbelievers were either directed to gods that don't exist (1 Corinthians 8:4), or remain unanswered by the Lord because he doesn't listen to the prayers of the unrighteous (Isaiah 1:15).

Even after the Holy Spirit has created new life in us through the gospel, giving us confidence to pray as children of God (Romans 8), Christian prayer remains a struggle, for we face the continuing opposition of the world, the devil and our own sinful flesh: we are tempted to manipulate God in a worldly way, as if he were our personal 'genie in a bottle', summoned to obey our commands; the devil will do all in his power to distract and discourage us from prayer; our sinful flesh is impatient when prayer doesn't procure from the divine superstore the delicious bargains we desire. The normal Christian experience of prayer feels like a spiritual tug of war, a relentless battle between God's Spirit and our sinful nature.

As Christians, we must fight to pray in the Holy Spirit's power. We can't indulge in self-pity, as if we were uniquely disadvantaged, for every Christian finds prayer difficult. But every Christian must pray. J. C. Ryle, the great Christian leader, wrote: 'Prayer is the most important subject in practical religion . . . Reading the Bible, listening to sermons, attending public worship, going to the Lord's Table [Holy Communion] – all these are very important matters. But none of them are as important as private prayer.' Prayer, Ryle explained, is the essential means of placing our faith in Christ for salvation. It is the surest mark of all the great men and women of God. It is the practice in which there is the greatest encouragement and the secret of eminent holiness. It is the best way of preventing spiritual backsliding and, indeed, of finding happiness and contentment.[1] Prayer is essential for every believer.

Where is help to be found?

Reading good books about prayer can help. There are many.[2] Even guilt can jolt us out of apathy. The intense shame of realizing that, if prayerless, I am the husband failing his wife, the mother neglecting her kids, the church leader betraying his congregation or the liar abandoning her friend – such shame can finally drive us to our knees. I noticed recently that my own godly father has pinned to the wall above his computer a sheet of paper with a simple rebuke to himself, 'PRAY, YOU FOOL!' Such spurs can help.

But there are usually more fundamental reasons for our reluctance to pray. When Jesus was asked by his disciples, 'Lord, teach us to pray' (Luke 11:1), he didn't rebuke or embarrass them. He taught them the Lord's Prayer.

The Lord's Prayer is what we need

There are some obvious reasons why this prayer is what we need. There is a story that the legendary golfer Jack Nicklaus would return annually to his golfing coach and ask him, 'Teach me again how to play golf'. He knew that he had to keep returning to the fundamentals of the game to try to master them, in order to carry on playing exceptional golf. Likewise, there are some basic principles of prayer to which we must keep returning. Like Jesus' disciples, we must go back to the Lord's Prayer and ask Jesus, 'Lord, teach me again how to pray'.

Among many reasons for studying this prayer, there are three that make it uniquely helpful:

This prayer comes from the Lord of prayer

Jesus is the ultimate prayer coach. As God, he knows exactly what kinds of prayer God will answer, and exactly what is wrong with our praying.

As the Son of God, he understands the privileges we now enjoy as the children of God. He knows how to approach the Father and please him.

As a man, he is sympathetic to the realities of our human condition. He knows what it is to feel crushed by responsibility or paralysed by fear. Like us, he has felt dog-tired and pushed for time. He knows our temptation to be lazy and self-indulgent. He is able 'to sympathise with our weaknesses', for he 'has been tempted in every way, just as we are – yet was without sin' (Hebrews 4:15). But he always made time for prayer.

Jesus practised what he preached. He was brought up in the Jewish custom of praying the *Shema* (beginning 'Hear, O Israel, the LORD our God, the LORD is one', from Deuteronomy chapter 6) and some version of the Eighteen Benedictions (traditional Jewish prayers) twice or even three times a day. He would have participated in the normal praying in the synagogue each Sabbath. We often read of him giving thanks at the beginning of meals, and for what the Father was doing through his ministry.

But the Gospels particularly emphasize his private, and often very extended, times of prayer. Mark records how, during a time of crisis, Jesus rose 'very early in the morning, while it was still dark', and 'went off to a solitary place, where he prayed'. Again, after feeding the 5,000, he went 'up on a mountainside to pray'. Once more, in the garden of Gethsemane, 'he fell to the ground and prayed' (Mark 1; 6; 14). Luke makes seven further references to Jesus praying, remarking that, 'Jesus often withdrew to lonely places and prayed' (5:16). Luke records him praying during his baptism, before Peter's recognition of his identity, on the mountain when he was transfigured, prior to teaching his disciples how to pray, and twice from the cross in death.[3] John further records Jesus praying before raising Lazarus from the grave, with a troubled heart while facing the hour of his suffering, and in his great plea for unity in the truth.[4]

Jesus was clearly a man of very considerable prayer. Both in regular personal devotions and in responding to situations of crisis, he constantly made the time to be alone with the Father to pray. It was hardly rocket science for the disciples to ask him, 'Lord, teach us to pray'. Jesus was the Lord of prayer.

As one who struggles with prayer, I don't want to learn from another failure. In the Lord's Prayer we have help from the expert!

Typically, the expert doesn't need to tell us endless rules and techniques, but can identify the fundamentals that we need to improve. As a very average rugby player, I recall one brilliant training session with Sir Clive Woodward, the World-Cup-winning former England rugby coach. He taught us more about rugby in one morning, by returning to the simple skills of passing a ball, than in countless previous training sessions put together. In the Lord's Prayer, Jesus has identified the few fundamental principles of prayer that his disciples must master. We need to return to them again and again.

There were obviously some aspects of Jesus' own praying that belonged to his unique mission. But the Lord's Prayer is his training for ordinary disciples like us. There is nothing in it that is unique to the special role of the apostles. It is true that, because he was speaking before his death and resurrection, Jesus left some of his phrases undeveloped. It is appropriate to enlarge our understanding of each phrase with the rest of Scripture. But part of the brilliance of the Lord's Prayer is its brevity. It is simple enough for children, yet can be easily expanded with biblical doctrine by mature Christians.

Jesus would not have prayed every part of the Lord's Prayer himself. He didn't need to ask for the forgiveness of his sins. He said, 'This, then, is how you should pray', not ' . . . how *I* pray'. For this reason, some have even suggested that it might be better described as 'the disciples' prayer'! (Indeed, there are some similarities between the themes of his prayer and some traditional Jewish prayers of the period. Jesus was probably perfecting a good contemporary model.)

All the themes found in the Lord's Prayer are, however, echoed in Jesus' own prayers. He customarily began by addressing God as Father: 'I praise you, Father, Lord of heaven and earth.' He prayed for the hallowing of God's name: 'that your Son may glorify you . . . ' He prayed for the kingdom to come: 'Father, I want those you have given me to be with me.' He prayed that the Father's will be done, even as he faced his crucifixion in the garden of Gethsemane: ' . . . May your will be done'. He thanked the Father for his 'daily bread', before feeding the 5,000 and at the Last Supper. Though he did not pray for the forgiveness of his own sins, he prayed for others: 'Father, forgive them, for they do not know what they are doing.' He prayed for our deliverance from evil: 'Protect them from the evil one.'[5] The Lord's Prayer plainly reflects what Jesus himself, as the model believer, commonly prayed.

As adopted children of God, Christians need to learn how to talk to our Father from our older brother, the Son of God, who has been doing it forever! He has given us his own Holy Spirit to help us pray in this way. This prayer teaches us the language of our new family. Learning from the Lord's Prayer is learning to pray from the Lord of prayer himself, our older brother and original Son of God.

This prayer is wonderfully flexible

A second reason for studying the Lord's Prayer is that it has so many applications for daily usage. From the different settings and wordings of the Lord's Prayer in Matthew 6 and Luke 11 it seems certain that Jesus taught this form of prayer on many occasions. Given the extraordinary scope of the prayer, this is hardly surprising. It is presented both as a 'model prayer', showing us exactly what form of words to use, and as a 'pattern for prayer', a flexible outline to adapt for different situations. In Luke 11, Jesus tells us to use his exact words: 'When you pray, *say* . . . ' This is not for use as a mindless mantra, but it would be perfectly proper to use exactly this form of words for heartfelt prayer on many occasions: in church, at the family dinner table or in private devotions. In Matthew 6, on the other hand, the Lord's Prayer is presented as a pattern for prayer: 'This is *how* you should pray . . . ' This is an outline to be expanded, a skeleton to be fleshed out. The Lord's Prayer is thus simple enough for 'baby' Christians to pray as it is, yet rich enough for older Christians to enlarge with further doctrine and applications to daily life ('festooning', as C. S. Lewis described it, or 'branching' as the Puritans called it). We will consider such applications in each chapter. Each phrase is a brilliant heading for masses of praying.

The New Testament letters contain many other prayers from the apostles that help us to expand on the themes in the Lord's Prayer. These tend to be more specifically focused on issues in the churches to which they were writing, whereas the Lord's Prayer is a general prayer for every situation. As we will discover, the principles found in the Lord's Prayer equip us for prayer in all circumstances. Moreover, we must remember that Jesus wasn't offering a suggestion but a command. This is how Christians *must* pray.

When we are spiritually dry, emotionally low or physically weak, this is a wonderfully simple format to go back to. I've found that Christians in hospital can say this prayer when they're far too weak for conversation. It's great for debate with unbelievers because it's familiar to many but rarely understood. I've found this prayer to be a brilliant subject for the talks and children's programme on a church weekend, for a men's convention, school assemblies and family prayers, where the children draw pictures for each phrase, and for private devotions. There are endless possibilities.

If we care about prayer, the Lord's Prayer will have the same sort of priority in our Bible study and ministry training programmes as we give to other primary doctrines. We need instruction in prayer, for, as Paul says, 'We do not know what we ought to pray' (Romans 8:26). Understanding the Lord's Prayer is a vital step along the road to maturity in prayer.

Since Jesus gave it to us, we can be sure that this is the kind of prayer that pleases God and the kind of prayer that he answers. We must stop assuming that God just wants us to pour out of our hearts everything that is in there. Being infinitely kind and long-suffering, he may tolerate many silly or selfish requests, rather as we might patiently endure the never-ending whining of a small child asking for sweets. But such behaviour is hardly acceptable in adults. We need to grow up, and the Lord's Prayer will show us how to pray maturely in all manner of different situations. This prayer is wonderfully flexible.

This prayer gives shape to life

A third great reason for learning from the Lord's Prayer is that it provides an extraordinary summary of the impact of the gospel on our daily lives. Through Christ, God is our Father (the opening address), our Lord (the first three petitions) and our Saviour (the second three petitions).

It is sometimes claimed that the Lord's Prayer concerns the future and that all the petitions are really requests for Jesus to return soon with the kingdom of God. There is some truth in this, for the six requests in the Lord's Prayer will be perfectly fulfilled only when Christ returns. Only when the King returns will our Father's name be hallowed by all, his kingdom welcomed by all and his will obeyed by all. Only when the King returns shall we be eternally satisfied, purified from sin, and safe from temptation and evil, to serve him perfectly in the new creation.

But the Lord's Prayer is also gradually being answered now. Jesus began establishing his kingdom during his earthly ministry, and the kingdom continues to grow today through the proclamation of the gospel. Our Father's name is already hallowed by many. His kingdom has already come, and is growing. His will is being done by Christians all over the world in the lives of his people. Believers enjoy the Father's provision of daily bread, pardon for sins and protection from evil. This is a prayer not only for our future, but also for God's children now as we travel through this world on our journey home. It is a prayer for the pilgrim people of God.

It is certainly a masterpiece – crafted with divine genius. The Bible commentator Matthew Henry called it 'remarkably concise and yet vastly comprehensive'. J. C. Ryle wrote, 'No part of Scripture is so full, and so simple at the same time.' The theologian A. W. Pink writes, 'Every part or aspect of prayer is included therein.' It has been called by other theologians a 'compendium of the gospel', a 'body of divinity' and a 'marvel of compression'.

The Lord's Prayer also crystallizes Christ's priorities for our whole lives. Jesus taught this prayer in his famous Sermon on the Mount (Matthew 5 – 7). Such prayer is part of the disciplined righteousness that he expects of his disciples that 'must exceed that of the scribes and Pharisees' and which we must seek first, above everything else.

Our prayers sometimes resemble a hastily written shopping list: a muddled selection of timid requests that reflect the self-absorption of our hearts and lives. This prayer brings fresh direction not only to our praying, but also to our living, for prayer is both the expression of, and the agenda for, our heart's desires.

It is only possible for Christians to mean this prayer. Even though the vast crowds at the funeral of Diana, Princess of Wales, joined in praying it, only Christian believers can truly call God their Father and want him to be honoured by all, his kingdom to rule over all and his will to be obeyed by all. Only Christians will consciously depend on God to provide our daily needs, to pardon our sins, and to protect us from temptation and evil. This prayer gives shape to the whole life of a Christian.

The Lord's Prayer has always been treasured by Christians

Being a form of prayer directly from the lips of Jesus, the Lord's Prayer has always been cherished and widely used by Christians. The *Didache*, a second-century Christian manual, recommends that Christians pray the Lord's Prayer three times a day! The early church leaders, Tertullian and Cyprian, commended its repeated use in private and public meetings. John Calvin and John Knox, the sixteenth-century Reformers, included it in their 'liturgies' after the sermon as a fitting response to the Word of God. Thomas Cranmer included it in the Church of England Prayer Book as an appropriate preparation for the sermon. Even the 'Directory' of the seventeenth-century theologians of the great Westminster Assembly, who were reluctant to advocate anything not specifically required in the Bible, wrote, 'Because the prayer which Christ taught his disciples is not only a pattern of prayer but itself a most comprehensive prayer, we recommend it also to be used in the prayers of the church.'

Christians at all stages and of all cultures around the world today use and treasure this remarkable prayer. But the public and private use of the Lord's Prayer has tragically declined in many Western churches, and it urgently needs to be revived. Its neglect has surely contributed to our problems with praying. The ancient language of some versions may have confused some, but modern versions are now readily available. Perhaps themes such as God's name, kingdom and will sound too heavy and impersonal, while asking for bread, forgiveness and deliverance today seems unfashionable. But Western Christians urgently need help to pray, and the Lord Jesus, our spiritual physician, commands us to take this prayer as the remedy for our spiritual sickness. We must listen to the one who wants us to meet God afresh as our Father, our Lord and our Saviour. When we begin to understand the Lord's Prayer and so to love his marvellous character and spectacular purposes, we will so enjoy him that we will want to pray.

Jesus gave us this prayer to help our praying. We would be incredibly foolish and arrogant to ignore his advice and so forfeit the intense delights of enjoying God in the Lord's Prayer.

'This, then, is how you should pray . . . '

2 'Our Father in heaven . . .'

(Being children of God)

The great British wartime leader Sir Winston Churchill was once famously chastised with the words, 'Winston, if you were my husband, I should flavour your coffee with poison.' With his usual lightning wit he replied, 'Madam, if I were your husband, I should drink it!'

Such words would be rude and cruel if they came from strangers, but they were in fact just friendly banter between Churchill and his long-time friend, Lady Astor. The way we speak to someone depends upon our relationship with them.

There is only one doctor I call 'Babe', and she is my wife. There is only one teenager who gets away with calling me 'Ugly Old Man', and he is my eldest son. There is only one little girl who begs to be carried on my shoulders, and she is my youngest daughter. The way we speak to someone depends upon our relationship with them. So it is with prayer.

People of different religions pray in very different ways, depending on how they picture the god they are praying to. Muslims repeat ritual prayers five times a day for a distant judge. Buddhists meditate silently upon their own inner being. Witchdoctors summon demonic spirits with ecstatic frenzy.

Roman Catholic nuns quietly intone the 'Hail Mary' using their rosary beads.

Jesus began the Lord's Prayer with the mind-blowing words, 'Our Father in heaven'. These words clarify the relationship in which Christians pray to God through Christ. Familiarity blinds us to their shocking impudence. The original Aramaic word for 'Father', *Abba*, was a term of respectful intimacy used in Jewish families, more respectful than 'Daddy' but more intimate than 'Father'; something like 'Dad'. Jesus tells us to begin our prayers by addressing the transcendent Creator, omnipotent ruler and terrifying judge of the cosmos as 'Dad'! What was he thinking? Among all the thousands of names invented for God by man, nothing remotely compares to the apparently blasphemous irreverence of calling the Supreme Being 'Our *Father*'. In the Jewish culture of Jesus' day, God was addressed with cumulative ascriptions of power and majesty. Jesus could have begun, 'Our Creator', 'Our Sovereign' or 'Our Judge'. Incredibly, he begins, 'Our Father'.

Jesus wants us to understand the extraordinary relationship we have as Christians with the God to whom we pray. We are God's adopted children. We are now welcome to approach him as our heavenly Dad, with affectionate and confident intimacy. Indeed, this is the whole context in which Jesus taught this prayer in his wonderful Sermon on the Mount. Even if Matthew's Gospel records only selected extracts from Jesus' teaching on that day, it is clear that the Lord's Prayer shares with the rest of Jesus' Sermon an emphasis upon our relationship with God as Father. Jesus refers to God as Father fifteen times in the Sermon. Our whole lives, including our praying, are to be lived not in a display of competitive religious performance motivated by fear of failure or pride in superiority, but with an attitude of childlike love and trust in our heavenly Father.

This little opening phrase contains all the motivation we need to pray. Like two Rolls-Royce jet engines strapped to a Ford Escort, the little words 'Our Father' are packed with power to launch us towards God in prayer. They summarize the miracle of God's grace in Christ, the whole message of Scripture, the heartbeat of Christian living, and the supreme glory of God. I'm convinced that most of our problems with prayer originate from a failure to comprehend these two little words.

The key to growth in prayer is not better technique, but better theology; not lessons in how to pray, but in whom we pray to; not meeting the 'prayer warriors' of history, but meeting our Father in heaven. Grasping this phrase transforms prayer from duty into joy, from pointless burden into daily delight. We need to know what it means to call God, 'Our Father in heaven'. We must start with Jesus, the original Son.

Jesus called God 'Father'

Jesus had three great reasons to call God 'Father' in his own prayers.

First, Israel was called God's 'firstborn son' (Exodus 4:22). In redeeming them from slavery for an inheritance in his earthly kingdom of Canaan, God gave them 'birth' as his children (Deuteronomy 32). They were given the privilege of calling God 'our Father' (Isaiah 63:16) (though there is little evidence that they ever did so). When Israel rebelled against God, he was grieved as a Father for his wayward son. But Jesus came as the perfect, sinless Israelite, entitled to call God 'Father'.

Secondly, the Messiah was called God's Son (2 Samuel 7). God promised a descendant to King David to rule for ever as a splendid king over his people: 'I will be his father and he will be my son.' This king would be enthroned with the royal title 'Son of God', for he would be as close to God as a son to a father (Psalm 2). When Jesus was raised from death to be enthroned at the right hand of the Father in glory, he was installed as this 'Son of God', the King. Jesus was this Messiah, the Son of God, entitled to call God 'Father' as the King.

Thirdly, Christ was eternally God the Son. When God became flesh in Jesus, he revealed himself as the second person of the Trinity, eternally related to the Father as the Son (though the Jews of Jesus' day recognized rightly that when Jesus addressed God as 'Father', he was 'making himself equal with God' and not his inferior, John 5:18). Jesus was the incarnate Son of God, eternally entitled to call God 'Father' as the Son.

So Jesus had three reasons to call God 'Father': he was the perfect Israelite, the promised Messiah and the eternal Son.

It is therefore no surprise to find that Jesus consistently addressed his prayers to *Abba*, 'Father'. All four occurrences of the word *Abba* in Matthew are instances of Jesus praying. In one prayer in John 17, we hear Jesus pray five times to *Abba*. Jesus was always praying to his Father.

Christians may call God 'Father'

Once we realize that this intimate language of fatherhood belongs in the first place within the heart of God himself, we begin to see what a glorious privilege it is to call God 'Father'. We are invited to pray as Jesus did, as children of the Living God. The great theologian J. I. Packer was in no doubt about the signific-ance of this:

> You sum up the whole of New Testament religion if you describe it as the knowledge of God as one's Holy Father. If you want to judge how well a person understands Christianity, find out how much they make of the thought of being God's child and having God as their father. If this is not the thought that prompts and controls their worship and prayers and their whole outlook on life, it means that they don't understand Christianity very well at all.[1]

We are not naturally God's children. Although the Bible teaches that all people are created by God, and are therefore in this sense God's 'offspring' (Acts 17:29), only the redeemed are truly his 'children'. Outside Christ, we are naturally 'objects of wrath' and 'children of the devil' (Ephesians 2:3; 1 John 3:10).

But by God's incredible grace, Christians are reborn by the Spirit of God through the Word of God and adopted into God's family: 'to all who received God's Son, to those who believed in his name, he gave the right to become children of God' (John 1:12). Paul wrote, 'God sent his Son . . . that we might receive the full rights of sons' (Galatians 4:4–5), and 'in love he predestined us to be adopted as his sons' (Ephesians 1:4–5).

This process of adoption was as familiar in Jesus' day as today. A wealthy but childless family might adopt a slave to carry on the family name. The slave was welcomed into the family as a new person, with a new name, cancelling all previous debts and giving him the right to inherit the estate.

The same is true of Christians, and much more. Believers are indwelled by the same Holy Spirit who indwells Christ and the Spirit unites us to Christ so that we may receive all he has accomplished for us. We are 'justified' in Christ (declared righteous with his righteousness), and also 'adopted' in Christ, that is, accepted with him into God's family to share all his privileges. The Holy Spirit continues to work within us to apply to our daily experience our new status in Christ, so that we gradually become like him and learn to pray like him. 'You received the Spirit of sonship. And by him we cry, "*Abba*, Father"' (Romans 8:15). As a newborn baby cries for its mother day and night, so born-again Christians will cry out to our heavenly Father in prayer.

Indeed, there are wonderful benefits enjoyed by all children of God:

We enjoy the tender love of God, 'as a Father has compassion on his children, so the LORD has compassion on those that fear him' (Psalm 103:13). In this love, the Father carefully provides for all our daily needs, pardons all our sins, protects us from harm, disciplines us in the way we should go, and showers us with daily blessings.

We enjoy the indwelling Spirit of God, the 'Spirit of sonship', who daily helps us to 'put to death the misdeeds of the body . . . because those who are led by the Spirit of God are Sons of God' (Romans 8:13–14). The Holy Spirit of Christ gives us birth into a life of loving worship of God, empowering us to know Christ, prophesy for Christ, grow like Christ, and serve the body of Christ.

We enjoy the comfort of the family of God as we are 'devoted to one another in brotherly love' (Romans 12:10). How often we are carried through tragedy and heartache by our brothers and sisters in God's family. How often we have cause to thank other Christians for support in the form of meals or money, secret prayers or public encouragement, teaching and practical assistance of every kind. Just as a good family will come running when any of the kids needs help, so often we find that when we cry out to God in distress, he doesn't remove us from our sufferings in this world but sends other members of the family into them with us, to help and strengthen us to endure.

We enjoy an inheritance in the home of God, for 'if we are children, then we are heirs – heirs of God and co-heirs with Christ' (Romans 8:17), sealed with the Spirit 'who is a deposit guaranteeing our inheritance' (Ephesians 1:14). As good parents try to ensure a secure future for their children, so our Father has prepared the most exciting future imaginable for us with him. We will inherit life in the renewed creation, the home of righteousness, where we will belong with our Father's marvellous multicultural family, sharing in his paradise 'rest' for ever. (It is because Jesus is the Son and therefore the sons in Jewish families were the heirs, that through faith in Christ male and female children of God are called 'sons of God' – we are all heirs!)

Finally, we enjoy the constant attention of God, for 'the righteous cry out, and the LORD hears them' (Psalm 34:17). As any decent father will hear and respond immediately to a child in distress, so God listens attentively to all our prayers. Our heavenly Father encourages us to call upon him at any time of day or night, for he never sleeps or loses interest. Indeed, because we are united to Christ by faith, when we are adopted into God's family we not only join the international people of God scattered around the world, we are even brought right into the triune family of God himself! When we pray, we are not shouting to our Father from a distance. We can whisper in our hearts to our Father, for as members of the body of the Son we have 'access to the Father by one Spirit' (Ephesians 2:18). In Christ by faith, we are praying from within the Trinity of God!

Even human fathers love to be contacted by their children, especially when they are away from home. Think of the moving publicity campaign by Fathers for Justice in the UK, wanting to raise public awareness of the desperate desire of dads separated from their partners to be given access to their kids. How much more does our heavenly Father want us to talk to him in prayer – not for his benefit but for ours, because he loves us? How it must grieve our Father, who sacrificed his Son, Jesus, to a brutal death in order to adopt us as his children, to find us so reluctant to pray. Surely our Father in heaven must want to say to each of us, 'I love you so much; don't you want to, just for a moment, stop talking on your mobile phone to people who can't help you and talk instead to *me*?'

With typical humility, Jesus does not even mention his own name in this prayer, even though he enables every blessing in it, especially in securing our adoption by the Father through his death. Jesus is the natural Son. We are the adopted sons who share in his privileges. So we will want to thank the Father for Jesus when we pray these words.

Christians share the amazing privilege in Christ of talking to Almighty God as 'Our Father'.

Life is now about pleasing our Father

In his Sermon on the Mount, Jesus outlines the Christian right-eousness without which no-one will enter the kingdom of heaven (Matthew 5:20).

Pleasing our Father is the dominant theme of Jesus' Sermon, as we see in the following: 'Let your light so shine before men that they may see your good deeds and *praise your Father in heaven* . . . Pray for those who persecute you that you may be *sons of your Father in heaven* . . . *your Father who sees what is done in secret will reward you* . . . *your heavenly Father knows that you need them* . . . how much more will *your Father in heaven give good gifts* to those who ask him . . . not everyone who says to me, "Lord, Lord" will enter the kingdom of heaven but *only he who does the will of my Father in heaven*' (Matthew 5 – 7, author's italics).

Christian righteousness is about praising our Father, becoming like our Father, seeking the approval of our Father, relying upon our Father, appreciating our Father, and obeying our Father – in other words, living for our Father, as did Jesus the Son. So when Jesus starts teaching about prayer, it's entirely consistent with the theme of his Sermon and his view of the whole Christian life, that his model prayer begins, 'Our Father'. This is what life is about now for the adopted children of God!

Jesus' teaching on prayer is flanked by teaching about giving (Matthew 6:2–4) and fasting (verses 16–18). Of course, adherents of many religions give, pray and fast, but Jesus distinctively teaches that Christians must do these things for our heavenly Father.

Jesus focuses on two particular features of Christian prayer. Again, both follow from the fact that God is our Father.

First, unlike religious 'hypocrites' who try to look impressive by praying publicly to gain popular acclaim, we are to pray privately for our Father's approval. When we learn from this prayer how wise and generous God is, we won't want to indulge in competitive religious showing-off but will want to get away privately to speak with our heavenly 'Dad'. As a wife would much rather receive flowers from her husband in private than in an extravagant public display intended to impress his mates, so also our heavenly Father wants us to talk to him in private.

Secondly, unlike idolatrous 'pagans' who try to manipulate God with endless babbling incantations, Christians can trust the Father to know what we need even before we've asked him. Prayer is not about getting what we want; it's about wanting what God wants for us and for others. As no husband appreciates being remorselessly badgered by his wife in an attempt to cajole him into accepting her incessant demands, so our Father wants us to trust that he does understand what we need without faithless babbling.

Furthermore, prayer is simply about being with our Father. When he says, 'Your Father . . . will reward you' (Matthew 6:6), Jesus does not specify the nature of the reward. Since Jesus has said that the hypocrite who prays publicly has already received his reward in the approval of people who see him, the implied reward of praying in secret is simply to enjoy pleasing and being with the Father because we want to be with him (rather than being 'paid' for our prayers when we get to heaven!). Private prayer removes from us the temptation to seek our reward in the approval of others. Just as a small child enjoys simply jumping onto her dad's lap for a hug, so also we enjoy the simple experience of being close to our heavenly Father in private prayer. Our Father is himself both the reason we pray and the reward we seek.

Since life is primarily about living for our Father, Jesus instructs us to begin our prayers with 'Our Father'. Some are in the habit of praying to Jesus or even the Holy Spirit. But we can be confident that prayers to the Father are known to all of the divine Trinity, since God is three persons in one God. We speak to the Father in the name of the Son, in the power of the Holy Spirit, for through Jesus we all 'have access to the Father by one Spirit' (Ephesians 2:18).

We say 'our' to remember the rest of the family

Jesus reserved the singular phrase 'my Father' for his own unique Sonship. But he tells us to use the possessive pronoun 'our'. This reminds us that, by his new covenant relationship with us, we are permanently adopted as his children. God has bound himself by Jesus' blood to be our Father. He is not just '*the* Father' in heaven, but '*our* Father'. He belongs to us. No-one can take him from us. He's given us the right to speak to him whenever we need him.

Supremely, however, this word is plural to remind us to pray for others in the family as well as ourselves. Nowhere in this prayer is there an 'I' or a 'me'. We are prone to pray selfishly, but Jesus instructs us to pray generously for the rest of God's family. As the great theologian John Calvin put it, 'There is nothing in which we can benefit our brothers more than in commending them to the providential care of the best of fathers.' We often feel unable to help our brothers and sisters in need around the world. But our Father is right there with them and delights to help them when we pray.

I have a friend who obeys this 'plural' by using a missionary diary called *Operation World*, which contains information about Christians in different nations for every day of the year.[2] He works successively through the diary, praying each day for Christians all over the world, as well as for friends and colleagues whose birthdays fall on that day. Apparently he prays for me and the people of Bangladesh on my birthday! The Lord's Prayer encourages us to put aside our selfish instincts and pray for others in our new family.

We say 'in heaven' to remember how great our Father is

Jesus tells us to pray to our Father 'in heaven' to remind us, not that he is distant (for he is close to everyone – Acts 17), nor that he is restricted (for he is everywhere – Psalm 139), but that he dwells in heaven which is high above us all, implying that he is immeasurably greater than we are. The Gospels record Jesus using the phrase 'Father in heaven' fourteen times. This form of address reminds us that our Father is the all-knowing, all-powerful, ever-present, invisible, immortal and unchanging supreme Lord of all. We are to be humble and not disrespectful. Perhaps we might even consider adopting a posture in prayer that expresses deep reverence rather than casual disregard for his eminence. It may seem appropriate to confess our sin on our knees or even on our faces.

Addressing our Father 'in heaven' (though he's spirit and can't be contained in such a tiny universe) reminds us that he is the Almighty God – unimaginably powerful and transcendently sovereign. For 'Our God is in heaven; he does whatever pleases him' (Psalm 115:3) – the perfect dad for sorting out tricky situations. Those who bully and hurt us will answer to him. Some kids boast that their fathers have fast cars or live in big houses or have important jobs. We can feel quietly secure in the knowledge that our Father in heaven owns all the cars and houses and everything else besides.

'Heaven' also reminds us of God's holiness. It is great to pray to the one who is not only powerful but also good with his power. Having recently watched the film *The Last King of Scotland*, Forrest Whittaker's award-winning portrayal of Idi Amin, Uganda's mass-murdering former president, I am reminded of how easily human rulers are corrupted by power. Thankfully we pray to an Almighty Father who is incorruptible. Dwelling in heaven, he is not only absolutely powerful, but also absolutely good.

This is an especially great joy to those with a negative experience of human fatherhood. Many people have not known their earthly father – he may have died or deserted them years ago. Other fathers are guilty of terrible abuse, leaving their children unable even to imagine a loving father. But we don't need to project the image of our deeply flawed earthly fathers onto our perfect heavenly Father. On the contrary, God is the one from whom human fatherhood derives (Ephesians 3:15), and he is far greater than even the best human father any of us has known. Those of us who lack, or have suffered under, a human father can find in our heavenly Father the loving Dad that we long for. Perhaps we'll appreciate him more than others ever can.

We say 'Father' to remember that he loves us

Human fathers often love us weakly or only when we succeed, behave or interest them, and only if they have the energy, time and sufficiently low alcohol levels. Our heavenly Father is quite different. The Bible reveals that, although we are more sinful than we ever realized, we are more loved by our Father than we ever dared hope.

Jesus emphasizes three magnificent aspects of the Father's love for each one of us:

First, the Father rewards our efforts to please him: ' . . . your giving may be in secret. Then your Father, who sees what is done in secret, will reward you . . . go into your room, close the door and pray to your Father who is unseen. Then your Father who sees what is done in secret, will reward you . . . wash your face so that it will not be obvious to men that you are fasting, but only to your Father, who is unseen; and your Father, who sees what is done in secret, will reward you' (Matthew 6:4, 6, 17–18). Though earthly fathers often fail to appreciate, or even rubbish, their children's efforts, our heavenly Father never fails fully to reward our loving service, now and in eternity, with himself.

Secondly, the Father knows all about us: 'your Father knows what you need before you ask him . . . do not worry about your life saying, "What shall we eat?" or "What shall we drink?" or "What shall we wear?" . . . For the pagans run after all these things, and your heavenly Father knows that you need them' (6:8, 31–32). Where earthly fathers struggle to know what their kids really need, and certainly cannot provide it all, our Father in heaven, who created and sustains us, knows exactly how we tick and what we need even when we're confused ourselves. He will supply whatever we need to become like Christ.

Thirdly, the Father loves to answer our prayers with good gifts: 'Ask and it will be given to you; seek and you will find; knock and the door will be opened to you . . . Which of you, if his son asks for bread, will give him a stone? Or if he asks for a fish, will give him a snake? If you, then . . . know how to give good gifts to your children, how much more will your Father in heaven give good gifts to those who ask him!' (Matthew 7:7–11). How foolish we are to neglect praying because we doubt that it's worthwhile. Even human fathers love giving gifts to their kids. I'll never forget the incredulous joy on my younger son's face upon opening his fourth birthday present to find a Buzz Lightyear toy. He was ecstatic, and I was thrilled watching his joy. How much more does our Father love giving us good gifts. Christians don't need to feel guilty about enjoying the good things we receive (assuming we're being generous towards our family, church, gospel ministry and the poor), 'for everything God created is good, and nothing is to be rejected if it is received with thanksgiving, because it is consecrated by the word of God and prayer' (1 Timothy 4:4–5). As the perfect Father, God loves to shower us generously with blessings.

Our Father is fantastic

Think of Jesus' description of the Father's character in his parable of the Lost Son (Luke 15). Human fathers are often foolish about discipline, cross about nothing and impatient with childish weakness. Am I the only dad to have lost it with the children and then regretted it? By contrast, Jesus describes our Father in heaven as wise and patient with the ungrateful son who left home. When we pray the Lord's Prayer we can thank him for his incredible patience with us.

Human fathers can be unfairly critical of the mistakes that children make. Am I the only father who has overreacted at the wreckage left by Cyclone Kids in every room? But our heavenly Father is compassionate and merciful to every rebellious child who repents. The only biblical description of God in a hurry is when he welcomed home his wayward son. When we pray the Lord's Prayer, we can thank him for his mercy.

Human fathers can be too selfish to listen, too tired to care, too busy to be present, too ignorant to understand and too weak to change anything. Am I the only father to have resented helping with French homework, or driven the children up the wall by watching football, or neglected to pray with them about their worries? I've even driven away from a holiday beach, leaving one of the children behind! By contrast, the Father in Jesus' parable is extravagantly generous when the lost son finally arrives home in a mess. We enjoy this generosity every time we pray the Lord's Prayer. What a great Father he is: never forgetful, never late, never grumpy or selfish, even when we fail to appreciate what he does for us every day. When we begin to grasp something of this incredible kindness and grace, we will start praying with the affection and confidence of little children.

I once heard my thirteen-year-old son giving his eight-year-old brother some shrewd financial advice. The younger boy was desperate to buy a new electronic Gameboy® with the latest game, 'Crash', on it. This was clearly a matter of life and death. Realizing that he didn't have enough pocket money to buy it himself, the poor boy had collapsed in total despair. His older brother then came up with a classic line that just about sums up their financial strategy for life: 'Just ask Dad!' I was no match for the heart-rending appeals that followed, and my son was soon enjoying his brand new game (much to the despair of his mother).

The Lord's Prayer begins, wondrously, in similar vein. Our older brother, the Lord Jesus, who has known the Father for eternity, is telling us from his own personal experience how to face life's challenges. 'Just ask Dad!' he says. Or, to put it in his original words, 'This is how you should pray: "Our Father in heaven . . ."'.

In the Lord's Prayer, Jesus teaches us in the opening address to . . .

ENJOY GOD OUR LOVING FATHER
AS HIS TRUSTING CHILDREN

So how might we pray this in practice?

Leaping down the bottom steps onto the station platform, Caz threw herself through the closing doors into the crush of grim-faced commuters just as the moronic electronic voice announced the obvious: 'This train is now ready to depart.' Caz was late again and already stressed from spilling coffee on her new jacket in the rush. The rest of the carriage returned to catching the latest Brad and Angelina gossip in their *Metros*. Caz pondered how to use her thirty-minute tube journey. She couldn't easily read the latest 'Potter' standing up – too heavy. Yet again she'd failed to read her Bible, but if she tried to read it now, her billion bookmarks would fall out (and embarrassment was a factor too). But she could pray. Everyone would think she was meditating (the other legal secs were all into that good karma stuff).
    Her church's recent 'Refresh' weekend had been big on the Lord's Prayer. She felt pathetic praying like this

– like her whole Christian life, really. But she was sick of failing and knew enough now to have a crack at the Lord's Prayer. Frankie had said that it really helps as a prayer pattern. She liked Frankie, her crazy but wonderful cell-group leader. So, hanging from an overhead strap, head squashed against a glass barrier in carriage no. 4 of the underground train hurtling along the Piccadilly Line from Arnos Grove to Holborn, at 7.49 am on 4 June 2009, Carol Jennings, two and a half years old as a Christian, closed her eyes and finally began to pray the Lord's Prayer to her loving heavenly Father . . .

'*Our Father in heaven,*' she began, remembering to pray about each word . . .

'Father, dear heavenly Dad, thank you for adopting me.

Thank you for sending Jesus so I could become your child and heir.

Thank you for your love and Spirit and family and inheritance and attention.

Thank you for caring, for rewarding, understanding and giving me good gifts.

(By the way, sorry for being such a rubbish pray-er – please help me learn) . . . Er . . .

'*Our Father . . .* Thank you for belonging to us for ever now; thank you for my church family and please look after them today and please bless Mrs. Lewis who's grieving for her husband and . . . and please bless Tony who's soldiering in Afghanistan and keep him safe . . . and please help our Mission thingy draw lots of locals to you . . . er . . .

'*In heaven . . .* Thank you that you are so awesome and amazing. I praise you that you are powerful and can do anything you want. (Please help me to worship you at work today by being patient with my boss. Father, he's so rude, but please save him anyway, Father) . . . er . . .

'Thank you that you're so good and holy, so please help me to be holy in the way I treat Guy this evening when we go for dinner. Please sort out if we should get married 'cos I don't want to hurt him, but he's so sweet, and help us to be self-controlled as I'm out of my depth. Please sort it out, Father.'

Caz was interrupted as the train shuddered to a halt at Turnpike Lane. A new mob squeezed in and, with a Kiwi backpack in her face, she was too uncomfortable to pray any more. But she vowed to return to the Lord's Prayer later. Praying to her Father had felt good, actually surprisingly good.

And meanwhile . . .

'Come on now, Milly'. Mike was trying to persuade his five-year-old daughter in fluorescent pink Barbie pyjamas to stop bouncing on the bed long enough to pray. 'Time for bed now. Let's say Jesus' prayer,' he suggested as she chattered away. Being on holiday in Sydney, Australia, her body clock wasn't right yet and she seemed worryingly awake. Even at home she could talk for an hour without ever taking a breath. 'Put your hands together now and close your eyes tight and let's begin . . . Our Father in heaven . . . ' he said, trying to establish some momentum.

'Daddy.' He was dreading the usual stream of theological conundrums.

'Yes, dear?'

'You're my daddy here and God is my daddy in heaven, isn't he?'

'Yes'. His biblical knowledge was about to be cruelly exposed.

'But if you have Mummy to help you, who does God have?' she asked, clearly hoping that another question about three Gods or one God could keep her father with her for ages.

'Well, God is one God in three persons: God the Father, God the Son and God the Holy Spirit.' She looked puzzled. He tried to look as if it was obvious and carried on, 'And if we trust in Jesus, then God lets us be part of his family and be his children like Jesus is, which means that God the Father looks after us.' He felt triumphant at getting a whole sentence out without interruption.

'So God is our Father in heaven?' She sensed an exciting new line of research.

'Yes, he lives in heaven and one day we'll go to be with him when we die, and until then he cares for us on earth, but we can pray to him now,' he replied, fearing the worst.

'But if we're down here and he is up in heaven,' she said, triumphantly, 'we need to shout or he won't hear us. *Amen!*' she yelled at the top of her voice, and then collapsed into a fit of giggles at her own brilliance.

'Ok, clever clogs, time for sleep,' he said, retiring from the ring gracefully.

'But Daddy,' she wailed, 'we have to pray Jesus' prayer.'

'Alright, alright,' he surrendered, helplessly. And together they said the Lord's Prayer, with his little pink angel shouting every word at the top of her voice.

When they'd finished, the poor man fled downstairs to report yet another defeat.

'I don't think this is working,' he confessed. 'I think the Lord's Prayer is too hard for her to understand.'

'No, no,' Sarah reassured him. She was instinctively shrewd about Milly. 'Every time you try and explain the words to her, even if she doesn't yet understand, she's learning to pray,' she reassured him.

'But how can she?' he protested. 'I hardly understand them myself!'

'But when you try to teach her the words, she's picking up from you that we pray because God is real, that he's good, that we need him and that you long for her to know him personally. That's discipling for five-year-olds! We need to keep praying with her like this until she understands for herself. Eventually she won't want to go to sleep without praying. One day, perhaps only in heaven, Milly will thank you for teaching her the Lord's Prayer.'

3 'Hallowed be your name . . . '

(Caring about our Father's reputation)

Until the sixteenth century, Western thinkers believed the astronomical theories of a scientist named Ptolemy from Alexandria. These included the view that the earth is located at the centre of the universe, and that all the stars, including our own sun, rotate around it. This theory flattered the human ego by apparently confirming our fond delusion that we are at the centre of everything. But in 1530, Nicolas Copernicus of Frauenberg Cathedral published his explosive discovery that the earth rotates around the sun. This was a colossal reversal of perspective. No longer could we proudly claim astronomical support for the idea that the universe revolves around us.

The Lord's Prayer demands a similar 'Copernican Revolution', shattering any foolish notions we may have about our own importance.

Consider its structure for a moment. After the opening address to 'Our Father in heaven' come six requests in two triplets. The first triplet appeals to Our Father as Lord. They ask for the extension of his sovereign rule over everyone, everywhere:

'Hallowed be your name' – may your character be
honoured by all;
'Your kingdom come' – may your rule be established over all;
'Your will be done' – may your plans be accomplished in all.

Notice the repetition of the word 'your'. These are clearly
requests for the advance of God's concerns in the world as our
sovereign Lord.

The second triplet appeals to our Father as Saviour. They
ask for our needs for life, both physical and spiritual, for now and
for ever:

'Give us today our daily bread' – provide the resources we
need for life;
'Forgive us our debts' – pardon our sins to save us from
your wrath;
'Lead us not into temptation but deliver us from evil' –
protect us from trials and from Satan.

This time the words 'our' and 'us' are repeated, highlighting the
fact that we need help from God as our Saviour.

The shock, the 'Copernican Revolution' if you like, is which
triplet comes first. Jesus puts concern for our Father before
concern for ourselves. This is not the way we generally want to
pray! Our natural self-centredness renders us far more concerned
for the provision of bread, pardon of sins and protection from
evil than for God's reputation, rule and plans!

But just as Copernicus discovered that the physical universe
doesn't revolve around us, so also we need to learn that spiritual
reality doesn't revolve around us either. We live in our Father's
world, and it revolves around him. Even the forgiveness of our
sins is less important than we thought. In the Lord's Prayer, we
can't pray about ourselves until we've prayed about God, and
we can't expect God to commit himself to us until we have first
committed ourselves to him.

This is a massive reversal. As self-absorbed sinners, we're fundamentally upside down about prayer. We like to think of prayer as our personal Aladdin's lamp by which we summon the divine genie to do our bidding: get me success, get me a partner, get me health, and be quick about it! We love the books and speakers that tell us that God just loves to hear all our problems and grant all our desires. When he doesn't we become cynical about prayer and about God. But Jesus teaches us that before we can know what to ask for ourselves, we need to learn what to ask for *him*. For when we think about his reputation, his rule and his plans, it will change what we then ask for ourselves. We like to think that prayer is primarily about getting God to submit himself to us, when it is primarily about getting ourselves to submit to him. Prayer is about joining our Father in his day before it is about him joining us in ours. We find this disappointing at first because we don't realize that we already live our lives in his presence. We find it boring to pray about God's priorities because we think they are distant and irrelevant, when, in fact, his plans involve all of our lives and our whole world as well.

Imagine a boy leaving school to start work in a factory manufacturing cars. It's hard work. He has a lot to learn. As the weeks pass, his father notices that his son calls him only at the weekends now. The boy doesn't hate his dad, but, to be honest, he just feels that his father wouldn't really understand and couldn't offer much advice because life in the factory is so alien to him. This lad rarely rings home these days and working life seems lonely. That is how most of us think of our lives in this world, and so we pray very little to God.

Contrast such reluctance with the situation where the Father owns and runs the factory. He has promised to teach his son the family business that he will one day inherit with his older brother! The son feels excited and privileged, daunted too, as he starts work and walks around the building trying to understand how the family business operates. He's eager to contribute in any way he can. He's constantly calling home, offering to help with his father's plans. Far from expecting his father to listen to his own inexperienced schemes, he's much more interested in his father's business – his reputation, his expansion and his plans.

So it is with prayer. When we start to realize that our Father's family business is the redemption and complete renovation of this world as an inheritance for us to share with Christ in glory, we'll be less obsessed with our own petty schemes and more excited about his reputation, expansion and plans. Prayer is not about getting our Father to stop what he's doing and fit in with our generally misguided schemes. Prayer is how we get involved with God's marvellous work in us and throughout the world. When we grasp this reversal of perspective, we will discover God answering our prayers in us and elsewhere! Nowhere is this more obvious than in Jesus' first priority in prayer, 'Hallowed be your name'.

'In the first petition . . . ,' explains the great eighteenth-century Westminster Shorter Confession, 'we pray that God would enable us and others to glorify him.' Another writer explains it as a request, 'that God's matchless name might be revered, adored and glorified and that God may cause it to be held in the utmost respect and honour, that its fame might spread abroad and be magnified'.

This request comes first because it should be the first priority of our Christian lives (just as it was for Jesus). All other requests flow from it. Frankly, however, if it wasn't in the Lord's Prayer I doubt if we'd ever pray 'Hallowed be your name' at all! So we plainly need to understand what God's 'name' means, then how to 'hallow' it, and, lastly, why we say hallowed be 'your' name.

Hallowed be your name!

To help us know him, God has kindly revealed himself in Scripture by his actions, his nature and his character, all 'fleshed out' in

Jesus. His character is revealed in his attributes (such as 'wisdom'), in images (like 'rock') and in wonderful names that paint portraits of him.

God's names reveal his character

Western culture does not generally use names to describe character. Names are chosen by personal preference, family tradition or, increasingly, to record a passion for a particular celebrity. In Britain in 2007, there were 4,000 babies named Keira (after Keira Knightley, the star of the *Pirates of the Caribbean* films), 1,600 called Britney (after the pop star Britney Spears), three David Beckhams (after the footballer), four Snoops (after a rap star) and six Gandalfs (perhaps the less said, the better).

Mind you, celebrities themselves seem to compete in choosing extraordinary names. Frank Zappa called his children 'Moon Unit' and 'Diva Thin Muffin Pigeon'. Bob Geldof called one of his daughters 'Peaches', Paula Yates called her daughter (with Michael Hutchence) 'Heavenly Hiraani Tiger Lily', Woody Allen called his son 'Satchel', Michael Jackson called his third child 'Blanket' and Helen Baxendale called her daughter 'Nell Marmalade'. I read recently of a footballer whose official name includes all eleven names of a previous Brighton and Hove Albion football team! Such names may register a loyalty, but they say little about the character of the child.

In Scripture, however, God gives himself many names to reveal his character, so that we may know and worship him. Two majestic names dominate the Old Testament: 'Elohim' and 'Yahweh'. Two more dominate the New Testament: 'Jesus' and 'Father'.

'Elohim' (translated 'God') means Creative Ruler

The name *El* stresses God's sovereignty. *El Elyon* means God most high, *Eloah*, God who is strong. The name by which God revealed himself to Abraham, Isaac and Jacob was *El Shaddai*, meaning 'powerful, able to bring the dead to life' (giving life to Sarah's womb). *Elohim*, the most commonly used name in Scripture, emphasizes the supernatural power of God (combining a word for reverence with a plural ending implying plurality and fullness in God). It emphasizes his power to create and rule us all. In the Lord's Prayer, Jesus tells us to pray that our Father will be honoured as *Elohim*, the almighty Creative Ruler.

'Yahweh' (translated 'Lord') means Faithful Redeemer

Speaking to Moses at the burning bush, God famously declared, 'I AM WHO I AM' (Exodus 3:14). This expresses the awesome truth that nothing prevents God from being who he is, and nothing stops him accomplishing what he wants to do. He then went on to identify himself as 'The LORD, the God of your fathers – the God of Abraham, the God of Isaac and the God of Jacob . . . This is my name for ever' (verse 15). The Hebrew word translated 'The LORD' in our English Bibles is pronounced 'Yahweh', and sounds like 'I AM WHO I AM' in the previous verse. This name reflects the fact that God's power is unlimited and unchanging.

The Lord then clarified how he would exercise his unfettered existence: 'I am the LORD, and I will bring you out from under the yoke of the Egyptians' (Exodus 6:6). This name emphasizes God's unrestricted freedom to be faithful to his promise to redeem his people from slavery. The name 'LORD' means 'Freely Faithful Redeemer'.

This name is then enriched further at Mount Sinai in sensational words to Moses, echoed many times in Scripture. The awesome glory of the Lord passed by Moses proclaiming his name, 'The LORD, the LORD, the compassionate and gracious God, slow to anger, abounding in love and faithfulness, maintaining love to thousands, and forgiving wickedness, rebellion and sin. Yet he does not leave the guilty unpunished; he punishes the children and their children for the sin of the fathers to the third and fourth generation' (Exodus 34:6–7). So 'LORD' means the 'Freely Faithful Redeemer who is both Merciful and Just'

(the death of Jesus would reveal how he can be both at the same time).

Further aspects of God's glorious character are revealed by additions to this name, 'Yahweh':

Yahweh-Jireh, a name revealed when God provided a lamb as a substitute sacrifice for Isaac, means 'the LORD provides' (Genesis 22);
Yahweh-Shalom, revealed in the victory given by God to Gideon, means 'the LORD gives peace' (Judges 7);
Yahweh-Sabaoth, revealed in the victories of Joshua over Jericho, David over Goliath and Elisha over the Arameans, means 'the LORD of victorious armies' (1 Samuel 17:45);
Yahweh-Rohi', revealed in David's famous Psalm 23, means 'the LORD is my Shepherd';
Yahweh-Tsidkenu, revealed in the promise of a king to rescue his people, means 'the LORD our Righteousness' (Jeremiah 23);
Yahweh-Shammah, revealed as restoring God's presence in Jerusalem, means 'the LORD is there' (Ezekiel 48).

Since the LORD is perfect and never needs to improve, he is all these wonderful things all of the time – his character is 'maximally alive' today and for ever: 'You made a name for yourself, which remains to this day' (Nehemiah 9:10).

This name stresses that there is only one God of this marvellous character: 'Yahweh'. He repeatedly proclaims to the nations, 'I am the LORD and there is no other' (Isaiah 45). Though people worship many gods that do not exist, whether the idols of Egypt and Babylon or the ideologies fashioned in the imagination of Western secular materialists, there is no God but this LORD.

Praying 'hallowed be your name' means praying that everyone will honour this freely faithful Redeemer who is merciful and just, Yahweh, the LORD.

'Elohim Yahweh' is *now* 'Father'

Through the saving work of Christ, the people of God may now call Elohim Yahweh 'Father', the 'Christian name' for God. As we have already seen, this name reveals the adopting love of God who cares for and protects his children and provides them with an inheritance in his eternal kingdom. Jesus tells us to pray that the Almighty Creating Ruler (Elohim) will be honoured as the Freely Faithful Redeemer who is Merciful and Just (Yahweh) and loved as our Father.

All these glorious names were most clearly revealed to us when God became a man.

Jesus is this God

The angel told Joseph about Mary's child, saying, 'you are to give him the name Jesus' [in Hebrew 'Yeshua' and in Greek 'Joshua', meaning 'God saves'], for he will save his people from their sins (Luke 1). God the Father chose this name for his Son because it summarizes his character and mission. It is the name of the leader who took Israel into the Promised Land, just as Jesus is leading his people into the promised eternal kingdom of God.

This name, 'Jesus' ('God saves'), summarizes all the previous names: Jesus is the Creating Ruler; Jesus is the Freely Faithful Redeemer who is Merciful and Just – our sacrifice, our peace, our victory, our shepherd, our righteousness and the presence of the LORD. Even the everlasting Father is revealed in his Son Jesus (Isaiah 9:6). All God's names are summed up in Jesus, for in him is the fullness of God.

Indeed, in Acts 3 – 4, the saving 'name' of Jesus repeatedly refers to Christ in all his power. Speaking to a man crippled from birth, Peter said, 'In the *name* of Jesus Christ . . . , walk', and the man was instantly healed. To the religious leaders, Peter explained, 'By faith in the *name* of Jesus, this man whom you see and know was made strong.' Hauled up before the rulers of Jerusalem the next day, Peter testified, 'It is by the *name* of Jesus Christ of Nazareth, whom you crucified but whom God raised from the dead, that this man stands before you healed . . . Salvation is found in no-one else, for there is no other *name* under heaven given to men by which we must be saved.' The elders decided, 'We must warn these men to speak no longer to anyone in this *name*.' So the believers called upon the Lord in prayer, 'Stretch out your hand to heal and perform miraculous signs and wonders through the *name* of your holy servant Jesus' (author's emphasis). In such contexts the 'name' of Jesus is not a magical spell but signifies him, present in power to save. When we pray, 'hallowed be your name', we are asking that everybody will recognize God's power to save in Jesus.

In words of breathless adoration, the apostle Paul explains that because of Jesus' self-humbling as our servant, obedient to the Father even unto death on a cross, 'God exalted him to the highest place and gave him the name that is above every name [i.e. God's own name], that at the name of Jesus every knee should bow, in heaven and on earth and under the earth, and every tongue confess that Jesus Christ is Lord [the Greek word for the living God who is Elohim Yahweh], to the glory of God the Father' (Philippians 2:9–11).

Everyone must eventually bow and confess the gospel that Jesus (the crucified man from Nazareth) Christ (the promised Saviour King) is Lord (the Risen Ruler and Returning Judge of all, who is God). God the Father will be glorified when everyone is raised up to bow before his Son, whether in adoration or in hostility, to admit that God's gospel is true and Jesus Christ is Lord. The name above every name, 'Lord', is now given to Jesus to exalt him for his self-sacrifice. He has become 'as much superior to the angels as the name [God's name] he has inherited is superior to theirs' (Hebrews 1:4).

There have been some powerful knees strutting this earth. But they shall all bow before Christ our Lord. The knees of all false prophets and influential gurus, the knees of all cruel despots and proud presidents, the knees of all wealthy billionaires and famous celebrities, the knees of all atheistic scientists and apathetic agnostics – all will bow in reverent submission before Jesus the Lord.

In the Lord's Prayer, Jesus tells us to pray that everyone will honour our Father, as he is revealed by his name, to be Elohim our Creator, Yahweh our Redeemer and Jesus our Saviour.

Now that we understand why we should hallow his name, let us briefly consider how we might daily do this.

Hallowed be your name!

We still use the word 'hallowed' of glorious sports arenas. We speak of the 'hallowed turf' of the old Cardiff Arms Park rugby stadium where Barry John, J. P. R. Williams and Gareth Edwards once revealed their mercurial genius, or of the 'hallowed arches' of the old Wembley Stadium where Moore, Charlton and Greaves wove their football magic. Such descriptions convey an expectation of respect and honour from everyone. How much more the name and character of God deserves to be cherished or 'hallowed'.

'Hallowed be your name' asks for the Father to be respected

When Jesus tells us to pray 'hallowed be your name', he is reminding us to ask our Father to ensure that he is worshipped as holy (literally, 'sanctified'), meaning adored with reverence, honour and respect, by everyone everywhere.

Of all the words used to describe God in the Old Testament, the adjective 'holy' occurs more often than any other. God is all of his splendid qualities, all of the time, and the word that summarizes his character in all its uniquely transcendent moral perfection and glory is the word 'holy'. This is the word that emphasizes how utterly different and immeasurably greater than us he is.

The heavenly beings could be impressed by many things about God, but Scripture says they are utterly consumed with wonder at his sheer holiness. In the vision given to the prophet Isaiah and again in the vision given eight centuries later to the apostle John, the mighty armies of fiery angels gathered in the presence of the Almighty are heard forever erupting in rapturous singing, 'Holy, Holy, Holy is the LORD Almighty; the whole earth is full of his glory' (Isaiah 6:3; Revelation 4:8). To 'hallow' our Father is to join these crowds delighting in the holiness of God with awestruck wonder. I've been present in the Millennium Stadium when the Welsh rugby crowds have filled their team and the arena with the tangible power and deafening roar of their passion. Yet this is but a faint whisper compared to the massed choirs of the heavenly multitude consumed with amazement at the dazzling holiness of God.

One day we'll join them, but, for now, such reverent 'hallowing' will be evident in our speech, behaviour and ambitions.

We ask for our Father's name to be hallowed in speech
In the Lord's Prayer, we pray that all people will speak with reverence for the Father. The Ten Commandments in the Old Testament made plain to Israel God's seriousness about the way people speak about him: 'You shall not misuse the name of the LORD your God, for the LORD will not hold anyone guiltless who misuses his name' (Exodus 20:7). One man openly broke this law, and was put to death: 'The son of the Israelite woman blasphemed the Name with a curse, so they brought him to Moses . . . Then the LORD said to Moses: " . . . anyone who blasphemes the name of the LORD must be put to death." . . . Then Moses spoke to the Israelites and they took the blasphemer outside the camp and stoned him' (Leviticus 24). Do we mock such severity?

When repeating the law to the next generation of Israel, Moses emphasized that this a zero-tolerance matter for God: 'If you do not carefully follow all the words of this law, which are written

in this book, and do not revere this glorious and awesome name
– the LORD your God – the LORD will send fearful plagues on you'
(Deuteronomy 28:58–59). Christians are no longer like Israel, a
nation with death penalties for law-breaking. But if we think
stoning was over the top, wait till we hear God sending people to
hell for the way they consistently spoke irreverently about him!

It is important to understand that the 'unforgivable sin' of
'blasphemy against the Holy Spirit' is not silly swear words
but failing to recognize the power of God in Christ (Mark 3).
The 'beast' of secular governments in Revelation 13 opens
his mouth 'to blaspheme God, and to slander his name and his
dwelling-place and those who live in heaven' by speaking against
Christ and his servants, whether in parliament or in the news-
papers. The blasphemy that offends our Father seems to be the
unbelieving scepticism and atheistic arrogance we hear from our
colleagues every day in the office. I recall being in our local gym
during a thunderstorm when one rather cocky lad opened a
safety door and shouted up to the sky to God, 'Is that the best
you can do?' He then turned to his friends expecting their
laughter. Unfortunately, his mates just looked rather nervous. I
think he will regret doing that.

At home, Christians will want to nurture reverence for God,
even gently in the informal prayers of children. Kids are unlikely
to believe in God if their parents speak of him as if he were a
mildly burdensome family pet.

In church, believers will want to ensure that our sermons, our
songs, our prayers and our conversations are not so casual as
to be disrespectful to God. At work, Christians will not join
in swearing, joking, criticism or rudeness toward our Father in
heaven any more than we would tolerate offensive words toward
our earthly fathers.

We will also pray and work towards respect for God in the
public arena. We will want God, Father, Son and Holy Spirit
respected in school and university classrooms. To be sure, we
will want to be as polite, law-abiding and diplomatic as God's

Word allows. But there are limits to what Christians will tolerate. When Shadrach, Meshach and Abednego were expected to worship an idol, they refused, and were willing to die rather than compromise (Daniel 3). Christians will likewise be unwilling under any circumstances to support or participate in 'multi-faith services'. Peter and John were commanded to stop speaking about Christ, but they refused, despite a beating, saying, 'Judge for yourselves whether it is right in God's sight to obey you rather than God' (Acts 4:19). Likewise, although as Christians we can agree to fulfil our employment roles properly without using evangelism as an excuse to shirk our responsibilities, we cannot undertake to stop speaking about Jesus for the hallowing of our Father's name.

We will also want to pray and work towards the hallowing of our Father's name in the media. The controversial musical *Jerry Springer: The Opera* was broadcast a few years ago on mainstream TV in the UK. In it, a choir constantly sings swear words, Jesus is depicted irreverently and there is blasphemous crudity throughout. No fewer than 55,000 Christians quite properly wrote to the BBC in protest. Most notable was the resignation of a senior BBC executive who publicly and graciously explained that he could not bear to hear his Lord, whom he worships and loves, so mocked and maligned.

More recently, the exhibition at the Baltic Gallery in Gateshead of a plaster statue of Christ in an offensive posture by a controversial Chinese artist understandably provoked a storm of protest from Christians who couldn't tolerate such irreverence towards God. The recent removal of the law of blasphemy in Britain is objectionable, not because the old law was good (in practice it had become unworkable), but because so few MPs or peers seem concerned about offending God. We must protest at blasphemy and irreverence towards our Father. We don't want laws against religious hatred that criminalize blasphemy (for unbelievers don't realize what they are doing). We do want the freedom to protest against the dishonouring of our Father.

And we want laws that forbid blasphemy against the glorious character of our Father (without criminalizing it). Jesus tells us to pray that it be so.

We ask for our Father's name to be hallowed in behaviour

We show reverence for the holiness of our Father not only in the way we speak, but also in the way we behave. As children of God, we show by our holiness what our Father is like and what his influence upon us has been. As one Puritan writer, Thomas Watson, put it, 'When our lives shine, his Name shines in us.' We will want to live in the holiness that brings respect to our Father.

We see this in human families. We speak of children being a credit to their parents or bringing disgrace upon the family name. Surely the lives of children bear more eloquent testimony to their parents than the finest autobiographies! Being children of God, we are our Father's promotional campaign, his advertisement in the world. If we live holy lives, reliable and honest at work, loyal to our friends, respectful in dating, supportive of our partners and caring towards our children, generous with hospitality and money, careful with alcohol, and kind to the weak and oppressed, others will quietly begin to respect our Father who has shaped our lives. But if we are dishonourable, argumentative at work, rude to shopkeepers, selfish with money, casual about porn or disloyal to colleagues, then others will think little of our Father. We 'hallow' his name by our behaviour.

A sad example of failing to hallow God's name is found in the pride of Moses in the desert. After the rebellion of the people of Israel at Kadesh Barnea who refused to trust God (Numbers 14), and then the rebellion of the leaders under Korah wanting positions of power (Numbers 16), we read of the sad rebellion of the great prophet Moses himself in striking the rock at Meribah (Numbers 20:10; 27:14; Deuteronomy 32:15). Instead of speaking to the rock to produce water for the people, as instructed by God, Moses struck the rock and then declared in frustrated pride,

'Listen, you rebels, must we bring you water out of this rock?' God says that Moses 'disobeyed my command to honour me as holy' (lit., 'hallow me'). For this he was condemned to die in the desert, without ever entering the Promised Land (though he went to be with Jesus because he appeared at the Transfiguration with him). God said to Moses and Aaron, 'Because you did not trust in me enough to honour me as holy [lit., hallow me] in the sight of the Israelites, you will not lead this community into the land I give them' (Numbers 20:12).

This is a warning for us all, and especially for church leaders, to be carefully obedient to God's instructions in his Word, to trust God to provide for his people as he has promised, without our needing to break his commands. We should be careful not to become proud and think that we are leading and providing for the church as equal partners with God rather than merely as his instruments and servants. Jesus is telling us to pray that our Father is hallowed by our behaviour.

We ask for our Father's name to be hallowed in evangelism

We hallow our Father's name, finally, in evangelism. The Bible is clear that God does not desire the death of the wicked, but that we should turn from our wickedness and live. Nevertheless, his primary motivation in saving sinners is the honour of his own reputation. Such an attitude in humans would be unbearably proud, but in God it is simply that when we are amazed by God's reputation, we enjoy him. God's glory is actually our blessing. As God reflects upon his redemption of Israel from Egypt, he says, 'I said I would pour out my wrath on them . . . But *for the sake of my name* I did what would keep it from being profaned . . . *for the sake of my name* I did what would keep it from being profaned among the nations . . . *for the sake of my name*, I did what would keep it from being profaned . . . ' (Ezekiel 20:8–9, 14, 22, author's emphasis). Nothing shows respect to our Father's name so much as people turning back to him in repentance and faith to rejoice in salvation and his glory. So evangelism hallows God.

As we proclaim the gospel, we advertise the name and character of God. As people submit to his rule and accept his salvation, his name is glorified and hallowed. Friendship evangelism, church missions, national campaigns and cross-cultural outreach commends to unbelievers the respect that our Father deserves, expressed in submission to his Son as our Lord and Saviour. Evangelism 'hallows' the name of our Father.

Our Father's name is our name

As a great family name bestows dignity and protection upon the family members, so the name of the Lord is given to his people as a blessing, for 'a good name is more desirable than great riches; to be esteemed is better than silver or gold' (Proverbs 22:1). There are some great family names: Churchill is an honourable name in England; Wallace is a great name in Scotland. To be a Bradman in Australia or a Tendulkar in India demands instant respect. One day, in the new creation, we shall all have the Lord's name inscribed permanently upon us as our mark of dignity and protection and belonging: 'They will see his face, and his name will be on their foreheads' (Revelation 22:4). We shall have the name of Elohim Yahweh Jesus Abba on our foreheads to mark us out as the special and beloved children of our Father in heaven for ever. Hallowed be that name!

Hallowed be *your* name!

Our wicked hearts love to be admired and respected. It is very striking that in the blockbuster film *Troy*, the motivation for mighty Achilles (played by Brad Pitt) in going to war to help Agamemnon recover his brother's beautiful wife, Helen, is the enduring glory of his name. The supreme motivation for so much human endeavour is the vain pursuit of personal glory, respect and adulation. Is this not the primary reason for the emergence of the celebrity culture in the West? We are taking the reverence and worship that rightfully belong to God and giving them to celebrity icons and then, like thousands of *X Factor* 'wannabes', longing for a little of his adulation ourselves.

Commentators sometimes fail to notice that the context of the Lord's Prayer is Jesus' condemnation of attention-seeking prayer: 'Be careful not to do your "acts of righteousness" before men, *to be seen* by them . . . when you pray, do not be like the hypocrites, for they love to pray standing in the synagogues and on the street corners *to be seen* by men' (Matthew 6:1, 5). Jesus is correcting the 'religious' reason for prayer to which our sinful hearts gravitate even after we're born of the Spirit of God. The first priority in his model prayer is to pray to win the admiration of others not for ourselves, but for God; not to have our own name respected, but out of respect for our Father's. How often do we organize public prayer to sustain and inflate our reputation as prayerful Christians? Jesus would have us immediately abandon any concern for our own names and surrender our hearts to praying 'hallowed be *your* name'.

Praising the name of someone worthy is enjoyable. It is no burden but a joy to be part of a crowd at a concert singing the name of Bruce Springsteen or Leona Lewis. It is thrilling to sing the praises of sportsmen like Rooney or Gerrard or Terry at Wembley. How much more is the 'hallowing' of God's name a delight to his children! Our Father designed us for pleasure in him. Since he is utterly good, he kindly created us to enjoy his goodness. God has so designed us that our deepest fulfilment and highest joy are in hallowing his name, and this serious duty coincides with our deepest delight. It's not that our Father is sinfully proud of himself or selfish for glory. But he knows that glorifying him is good for us as well as what he deserves. Learning to hallow his name will bring us the happiness we desire, and give us an intoxicating taste of heaven. Praying 'Hallowed be your name' is how we begin.

As a first priority in the Lord's Prayer, Jesus teaches us to enjoy God as our sovereign, redeeming, saving Father, i.e.

ELOHIM YAHWEH JESUS ABBA . . .
. . . AS REVERENT WORSHIPPERS

So how might we pray this in practice?

Caz sat alone at her desk, glad of some respite after a frantic morning. The others had popped out for sandwiches and, having bought pasta salad at Tesco, she savoured a few moments alone. The boss had a massive trial coming up next week, and Andy, the assistant solicitor, was clearly feeling the strain. He'd been rough all morning with all the legal secretaries. He was from a posh background, but he swore like a trooper. Caz didn't mind the crudity so much as the blasphemy; Andy must have shouted 'Jesus Christ' a dozen times that morning, and he wasn't singing Delirious praise numbers.

Caz took out her shiny new study Bible. She'd bought it at Refresh. Frankie said it had all the answers. She read the next paragraph in Mark's Gospel and paused for thought. She decided to carry on with the Lord's Prayer.

'*Our Father in heaven, hallowed be your name . . . er . . .*' (She'd found the talk on God's names a bit confusing but she remembered the big four.)

'I praise you that you are Elohim, our sovereign Creator.

I praise you that you are Yahweh, our Freely Faithful Redeemer.

I praise you that you are Jesus our Saviour.

I praise you that you are Abba, our Father, who has adopted us.

I praise you Elohim, Yahweh, Jesus, Abba – you really are amazing, Father!

'Er . . . Please help me to "hallow" your name and earn respect for you in the way I speak and behave and evangelize – especially here at work, Father. Please help me to "hallow your name" and bring you respect in my family (please help my flatmate Jo to start respecting you too). Please help Andy to stop using Jesus' name so rudely and may more people respect you in this office. (Father, I don't want to seem judgmental or fanatical, but, please give me courage and an obvious chance to ask him nicely to stop and to explain about Jesus. Help him become a Christian . . . er . . . Please help people all over the world hallow your name and learn to respect you as Elohim, Yahweh, Jesus, Abba.'

The lift bell rang and Caz knew that the others were coming back. 'J . . . C . . . , that took forever,' shouted Andy, bursting into the office like a foul-mouthed cyclone.

Caz swallowed hard. 'Andy,' she began sweetly . . .

And meanwhile . . .

Harold gobbled his doughnut as quickly as possible. The others at the table were taking ages. Betty gripped her mug of coffee tightly to get some warmth into her frozen fingers. Harold just loved this group, all gnarled and ponderous old veterans like himself. They'd all seen better days but had great stories to tell, of growing up in wartime Britain, of the Beatles and Bobby Moore and endless stories about the grandchildren. And of God too. Audrey had been a missionary with Africa Inland Mission. Fred and Lois, the only surviving couple (the others were all widowed except Audrey, who'd never married), had for thirty years run a shelter for the homeless in the centre of Leeds. Each had their own tale to tell of God's grace. They moaned a bit. But then, like Harold, they'd buried many loved ones and they suffered constant aches and pains. Indeed, Gerald looked as if he was on his last legs. But Harold had also seen their spirits soar recently as they'd begun to study the Lord's Prayer.

When Harold had begun leading this Seniors' Group, he'd discovered that they liked to see themselves as the prayer engine of St Ethel's. 'Invisible but Unstoppable' was their motto, according to Betty. And they did pray. Every week, same time, same table at the Seniors' Prayer Lunch, they'd pray for all kinds of things. Harold knew that the Father honours such faith in frailty.

'Right, everyone,' Harold had to speak up for Dennis. 'We're carrying on with the Lord's Prayer, using Derek Prime's book.'

'It's "Hallowed be your name" today,' said Lois, always keen to help.

'Did you all read Revd Jack's notes for today?' asked Harold.

They were usually pretty dedicated.

'Nothing original, but all good stuff,' said Fred. 'I've always thought Calvin's chapter on prayer was the best.'

'Revd Jack's only young. Give him a chance,' said Lois brightly. 'What now, Harold?'

'Well, let's pray for God's name to be hallowed in our lives, then in the life of the church, then in our country, and finally in all nations – about ten minutes for each section?' suggested Harold.

'What passage are we reading?' asked Doris bluntly, keen not to waste time.

'Exodus 20:7 and Philippians 2:5–11.'

'Know them off by heart,' said Fred. 'It's best in the King James,' he chuckled.

And so they read and prayed, struggling to be heard but full of the Spirit. The good people of St Ethel's would have blushed to hear these ancient saints praying for them. They praised Elohim their Creator, Yahweh their Redeemer, Jesus their Saviour, and the Father their Provider in reverent and measured tones. They prayed for the CYFA teenagers, that their relationships with friends and behaviour at school would earn respect for God. They prayed about the lyrics of Salt, the church rock group, for the kindness of the bereavement team and for the evangelistic preaching of the vicar. They prayed about the language used in TV programmes, government religious legislation, and the witness of Christians in Muslim countries, asking that the Father's name be hallowed everywhere. Harold had to stop them or they'd have carried on for hours (though Fred had fallen asleep and was snoring loudly).

'Right, next week is "Your kingdom come",' said Harold.

'Really? How exciting!' said Audrey, rather confused. 'I thought King George was dead?'

4 'Your kingdom come . . .'

(Caring about our Father's rule)

Praying for our Father's kingdom to come may seem strange. Why would we want a kingdom? Most Western monarchies were replaced by parliamentary democracies long ago, and a kingdom sounds like an unwelcome return to medieval tyranny. Modern Western governments may be disappointing, but at least we don't suffer the kind of persecution faced by our brothers and sisters under absolute monarchies such as in Saudi Arabia and Oman. Perhaps we should also admit that a patriarchal kingdom hardly sounds enjoyable – full of serious ceremonial and stifling royal protocol!

We need to take a guided tour of the kingdom of God in Scripture, to stroll along its cosmopolitan boulevards, explore its leafy parks and admire the historic architecture to catch a glimpse of what it's really like. We'll discover that God's kingdom is a paradise home that makes the Caribbean seem like wartime Stalingrad! The heavenly Jerusalem is a glittering city that's infinitely more exciting than New York, more relaxing than Sydney, more fascinating than Istanbul, more beautiful than Prague, more glamorous than Milan, more ancient than Beijing and more fun than London. And, best of all, God is there. Once we grasp the biblical picture of the kingdom of God, we'll be begging our heavenly Father, 'Your kingdom come'!

We pray to the King

God has always been the King. He is 'the great King over all the earth' and he alone is King, 'the blessed and only Ruler, the King of kings and Lord of lords, who alone is immortal and who lives in unapproachable light' (Psalm 47:2; 1 Timothy 6:15–16).

The King of kings rules everything according to his unchanging plans: 'the plans of the Lord stand firm for ever, the purposes of his heart throughout all generations' (Psalm 33:11). Indeed, he 'works out everything in conformity with the purpose of his will' (Ephesians 1:11). The King directs all of nature and history in every detail. He effortlessly upholds and directs the entire universe: every miniscule movement in every atom in every far-flung star, every beat of our hearts, and every moment of our personal lives and salvation. Even the decisions and choices we make are enabled entirely by the King and woven into the fabric of his plans.

This may come as an unwelcome shock to many. We like to think we run our own lives without God. We're rather like the tiny East Sussex hamlet of Ashhurst Wood in England, which on 1 January 2000 declared itself independent from UK government and taxation. The People's Republic of Ashhurst Wood Nation State ('PRAWNS' for short) wrote to the Queen and Tony Blair to declare their independence, drafted a constitution, organized checkpoints on the road to East Grinstead with a retired army colonel overseeing the defences, and issued passports and visas. Eventually this rather amusing rebellion collapsed. They couldn't issue visas fast enough for all the milkmen and postmen required! Our rebellion against God is equally doomed but has far more serious consequences. If we spend our lives rebelling against God and his gospel, we are choosing an eternity in hell and no-one is laughing there. God is our King, whether we like it, or not.

God the Father has always intended to exercise his kingship through God the Son. In the year that the great King Uzziah died (740 BC), Isaiah was given an overwhelming vision of 'the Lord seated on a throne, high and exalted . . . the King, the LORD Almighty' (Isaiah 6). Ruling in absolute power, this King is later identified by John: 'Isaiah said this because he saw Jesus' glory' (John 12:41).

God the Father wanted especially to glorify his Son by giving him a kingdom of redeemed people enjoying his sensational grace. So his Son voluntarily went to the cross to ransom us from death and sin and bring us into his kingdom. Then the Father raised and enthroned his Son in triumph as King for ever. The Father is now bringing all things in heaven and earth together under Christ's rule, as is demonstrated in Christ's church (Colossians 1:13; Ephesians 1:10). One day, the Father will send Christ finally to subdue his enemies, gather his people, renew his creation and establish his glorious kingdom for ever under his Father's rule.

We gain a mouth-watering picture of the nature of this fabulous kingdom if we explore its development throughout the Scriptures. Here is a whirlwind tour, so buckle up – it will take your breath away!

We pray for God's kingdom

To fully grasp the splendour of God's kingdom, we must start at Genesis.

In the beginning, God created a garden
Our Father fashioned the cosmos with a paradise garden kingdom where Adam and Eve could enjoy God's presence in obedience to his Word. But our ancestors rebelled (as we would also have

done) in an appalling display of sceptical, proud disobedience. Expelled from the garden, and, without access to the tree of life, they and all their descendants are now condemned to live and die outside God's kingdom. Genesis 1 – 11 records how the human wickedness that began in the garden descended into murder, provoked a cataclysmic flood from God, and finally gathered humanity together to construct the Tower of Babel in a crazy attempt at self-glorification. This introduction to Scripture reveals why we all need a Saviour.

When we pray 'Your kingdom come', we are asking to live in God's paradise garden.

God promised Abraham a blessed nation

With amazing generosity, God promised Abraham a land, a people and blessing through which he would bless all nations. This promise of the kingdom of God was later described by the apostle Paul as 'the gospel' (Galatians 3:8). Genesis records how Abraham's family were preserved through infertility, sin and famine to become a great people sheltering in Egypt. Exodus tells how this nation was blessed with redemption from slavery by God's power and from judgment by God's Passover sacrifice, to worship God at Mount Sinai. Again, God blessed them with his Word in the law, his presence in the tabernacle, and a sacrificial system (explained in Leviticus) to enable them to be purified for life in fellowship with him. Numbers describes how the Lord led Israel through the desert towards the beautiful Promised Land, suppressing the rebellions of the people, the leaders and finally Moses himself, and sending terrifying judgments that stand as a warning for us on our own journey to our future inheritance. Deuteronomy explains how Moses prepared Israel to enter the kingdom and live under God's rule in Canaan. These five books of Moses are used by New Testament writers to explain how Christians are ransomed from captivity into God's kingdom.

At a time when the British government seems intent on passing legislation that supports sexual immorality and abortion, while suppressing the Christian faith, we pray 'Your kingdom come' to express our longing to live under the loving and righteous laws of God, as lived and taught by Christ, in the beautiful promised land of heaven.

The history of Israel paints a portrait of a King

The history of Israel (Joshua to 2 Chronicles) describes various leaders who were appointed over God's kingdom. In combination, their noblest features paint a hugely impressive and attractive picture of a King repeatedly promised by God.

Joshua (the Hebrew word for 'Jesus', which means 'God saves') led God's people into battle against the enemies of God to conquer and inherit in the fertile land of Canaan, just as God had promised.

Judges such as Gideon and Samson were not elderly lawyers in wigs, but heroic spirit-filled warriors raised up by God to rule his people and rescue them from invaders.

God provided a 'kinsman–redeemer' called Boaz to enable Ruth, a foreign widow, to share in the blessings of the kingdom. She joined the family ancestry of the great King David and Jesus after him, to demonstrate the role of Israel in welcoming all nations into the kingdom of God.

Samuel was a great prophet and judge whose words from God governed the people of Israel and brought them his blessing.

When Israel pleaded for a king to fight their battles for them (rejecting God because they wanted to be like other nations), God patiently gave them Saul, David and Solomon whose combined strengths pointed to the future.

The first 'anointed king' (or 'Christ') was Saul. He was chosen by God, anointed with oil, filled with the Spirit and victorious in battle. But he disobeyed God and was replaced by the warrior, David.

Though he was despised by many, David won a great victory for Israel over the Philistine giant, Goliath. He humbly welcomed

God's Ark-throne into his capital. He was promised a descendant to rule for ever over God's kingdom, and wrote many beautiful psalms about this king. But David sinned terribly with Bathsheba and was replaced by Solomon.

Solomon (whose name means 'Peaceful') ruled with famous wisdom, established peace and prosperity, and built a temple for the Lord to dwell among his people so he could rule, bless and forgive them. On visiting Israel during Solomon's reign, the exotic Queen of Sheba was absolutely staggered by the happiness and prosperity of the nation under God's king.

The promised King would be greater than all these rulers combined. We become particularly aware of our desperate need for this King when we struggle to govern our own lives well or suffer under the foolish leadership of others. When we pray 'Your kingdom come', we ask our Father to send this marvellous King who will lead us into our inheritance as Joshua did, deliver us from enemies as Samson did, pay for our immigration as Boaz did, teach us God's Word as Samuel did, be anointed with God's Spirit as Saul was, be victorious and humble after God's own heart, like David, and be a wise governor who brings us security and joy in God's presence, like Solomon.

The prophets promised a spectacular new kingdom

Solomon's heart was tragically led astray by his many pagan wives and concubines. Under God's judgment, the kingdom of Israel was torn apart by civil war. The northern kingdom was ruled by godless kings and the Lord sent the Assyrians to destroy it in 722 BC. The southern kingdom was little better, and God raised up the Babylonians to destroy Jerusalem and take his people into exile in 586 BC. The kingdom of God seemed to have collapsed.

But the Lord sent prophets both to declare his judgment and promise a spectacular new kingdom. They spoke of a renewed Temple, Jerusalem, Land and Creation. They spoke of a vast, international, resurrected people. They spoke of another great redemption from exile. And they promised the great King, Prophet, Priest, Judge, Kinsman-Redeemer, Shepherd, Son of Man and Suffering Servant who would rule for ever. Isaiah proclaimed that this King would be God himself: '"Here is your God!" See the sovereign LORD comes with power . . . He tends his flock like a shepherd: He gathers the lambs in his arms and carries them close to his heart' (Isaiah 40:9–11). The splendour of his kingdom would dwarf the glories of the Egyptian, Chinese, Inca, Greek, Roman, Spanish, British, Soviet and American empires combined. This is the fabulous kingdom for which we pray in the Lord's Prayer, and it will be breathtakingly wonderful.

God urged the exiles to wait for God's kingdom, such as Daniel, who resolved not to defile himself in a pagan land (Daniel 1:8), because 'the Most High is sovereign over the kingdoms of men' (Daniel 2 – 7). A small remnant of Israel returned to rebuild Jerusalem under Ezra and Nehemiah, but God's people still longed for the glorious kingdom promised by the prophets.

There was silence from God for four centuries. The question on the hearts of all faithful Israelites was 'Where on earth is God's spectacular kingdom? And where is his promised king?'

This silence was finally broken by the prophet John the Baptist, who emerged to warn everyone to repent in preparation for the imminent arrival of the great King ' . . . whose sandals I am not worthy to stoop down and untie' (Mark 1:7).

Then, at last, the long-awaited and momentous day dawned when a tradesman from Nazareth announced in words of staggering significance, 'The time has come . . . The kingdom of God is near. Repent and believe the good news!' (Mark 1:14). The King had arrived.

Jesus is God's King

Many expected this king to rescue Israel from Roman occupation. But Jesus proclaimed a far greater deliverance: liberation from sin, Satan and death. Quoting the prophet Isaiah, he declared in the synagogue in Nazareth, 'The Spirit of the Lord is on me, because he has anointed me to preach good news to the poor. He has sent me to proclaim freedom for the prisoners and recovery of sight for the blind, to release the oppressed, to proclaim the year of the Lord's favour' (Luke 4; compare Isaiah 61). He then announced to his stunned audience that this promise had finally been fulfilled. He was the King, and they were among the captives needing liberation.

Jesus demonstrated the power of his rule in his teaching, his miracles and his death.

The crowds were astonished by the power of his teaching: 'The people were all so amazed that they asked each other, "What is this? A new teaching – and with authority!"' (Mark 1:27). The dominant theme of his preaching was the kingdom of God. He spoke of how it grows in the world through the gospel, like seed sown in a field. Though fruitful only in some, unimpressively small and frustratingly slow, this gospel seed will eventually produce a massive harvest of people for God's kingdom. He spoke of how the King would be hated, his invitation to the kingdom banquet scorned, his Son killed by the tenants of the vineyard, and the cornerstone of his household discarded. He spoke of how lowly outcasts, guilty tax collectors, lost sheep and rebellious sons could be forgiven and welcomed into his kingdom. And he spoke of how he would return in power to judge, like a returning king coming to reward his faithful supporters but crush his enemies. His teaching remains self-evidently true because he is the divine King who speaks the truth with the compelling personal authority of God.

His royal power was further demonstrated in miracles. In one day, Jesus calmed a furious storm, delivered a man possessed by demons, healed a woman with incurable 'bleeding' and raised Jairus' daughter from the dead (Mark 4 – 5). In each case the inadequacy of human power is emphasized. But Christ ruled with ease over nature, demons, disease and death, demonstrating some of the blessings of life in the new creation of his coming kingdom.

The royal power of Jesus was shown supremely in his death. He rode into Jerusalem on a donkey as a humble sovereign, to be our suffering servant. He was tried and condemned for blasphemy and treason for claiming to be the divine King. In answer to the question, 'Are you the Christ, the Son of the Blessed One?', he freely declared, 'I am . . . And you will see the Son of Man sitting at the right hand of the Mighty One and coming on the clouds of heaven' (Mark 14). The High Priest tore his clothes, for Jesus had plainly declared himself the divine King. Lifted up in glory on the cross, he was nailed under a sign proclaiming him King. He promised the repentant thief who hung next to him a place in his paradise kingdom. He emerged from the bloody battlefield of the cross as the victorious conqueror of Satan, sin and death, tearing down the gates of hell to rescue his people for his kingdom. Now enthroned at the right hand of God, our King continues to rule over his people through his Word, interceding for us before our heavenly Father.

When we pray 'Your kingdom come', we are asking our Father to rule over us through Jesus, our scarred Saviour and caring King. We are welcoming his laws, trusting his power, celebrating his triumphant death and expressing our deep longing to see him face to face in glory. We pray, 'Our Father . . . please send Jesus, your magnificent King'.

The apostles preached this kingdom. Philip 'preached the gospel of the kingdom of God'. Paul 'declared . . . the kingdom of God . . . and tried to convince them about Jesus'. Again, 'boldly and without hindrance he preached the kingdom of God and taught about the Lord Jesus Christ' (Acts 8; 28). The gospel of the kingdom is not separable from the gospel of Christ crucified. The death of the King opened the way for his subjects into his coming kingdom.

The apostle John was given a glorious vision of life in this kingdom (Revelation 21 – 22), a travel brochure for Christians on their way to eternal rest with Jesus. John saw a resurrected creation, with a sparkling new Jerusalem, a sumptuous new garden and a refreshing river flowing with the water of life (symbolizing the life-giving Holy Spirit). He saw the tree of life (symbolizing the cross) with leaves for healing and sustaining the nations. The curse resulting from Adam's sin had been removed, exhausted by Christ on the cross. Those who have 'washed their robes in the blood of the lamb' can look forward to being comforted personally by God, and will enjoy serving him perfectly, seeing him clearly, and reigning over the new creation with the Lord Jesus Christ. God Almighty and his enthroned Lamb will dwell with us for ever and we will finally be the people he wants us to be.

'Your kingdom come' means that we long for the kingdom of the renewed creation promised in Scripture.

We are praying for evangelism

We pray 'Your kingdom come' precisely because God's kingdom has not yet arrived. However, when we become Christians, we surrender our lives to the King. We become citizens of the heavenly kingdom of God, in the sense that we have submitted ourselves to the rule of Jesus our King, so 'our citizenship is in heaven' (Philippians 3:20). This explains why Jesus could say to his disciples, 'the kingdom of God is within you' (Luke 17:21), and yet declare to Pilate, 'My kingdom is not of this world . . . my kingdom is from another place' (John 18:36), and to Nicodemus, 'No-one can see the kingdom of God unless he is born again' (John 3:3).

This helps us clarify some misunderstandings about God's kingdom. God is not building a paradise kingdom within this world, as Jehovah's Witnesses believe. Christ will not return to the earthly Jerusalem to establish his kingdom within the land of Israel, as Zionists and Dispensationalists believe. God is not establishing his kingdom in this world by liberating people from social deprivation and oppression, as many Liberation Theologians believe.

Christians have always been involved in mercy ministries to those in hardship in this world, but this doesn't extend the kingdom of God unless people repent and surrender their lives to the King. The kingdom of God is not of this world, but of heaven.

Of course, the citizens of heaven will want to live lives shaped by the values of the King and his coming kingdom. When citizens of the United Kingdom travel abroad, they commonly exhibit a passion for the special joys of British culture. The citizens of this earthly kingdom will go to bizarre lengths to find fish and chips, warm beer and bingo, even in a tropical climate! Citizens of the kingdom of God will hopefully display more attractive features of our heavenly culture. By exhibiting the values of heaven, we attract unbelievers to join us in submission to our heavenly King.

As Rodney Stark observes in *The Rise of Christianity*, the church has given birth to a heavenly counter-culture from its earliest days:

> Christianity revitalized life in Greco-Roman cities by providing new norms and new kinds of social relationships able to cope with many urgent problems. To cities filled with the homeless and impoverished, Christianity offered charity as well as hope. To cities filled with newcomers and strangers, Christianity offered an immediate basis of attachment. To cities filled with orphans and widows, Christianity provided a new and expanded sense of family. To cities torn by violent ethnic strife, Christianity offered a new basis for social solidarity. And to cities faced with epidemics, fire, and earthquakes, Christianity offered effective nursing services . . . for what they brought was not simply an urban movement, but a new culture capable of making life in Greco-Roman cities more tolerable.[1]

The culture of our Father's kingdom follows wherever the gospel is heard and the King obeyed. Unbelievers witness the invasion of the kingdom of darkness by the kingdom of God, and are drawn to the King.

This glorious truth is sometimes acknowledged in unlikely places. The atheist commentator Matthew Parris wrote an article in *The Times* in December 2008 with the headline, 'As an atheist, I truly believe Africa needs God.' This observation, he concedes, 'stubbornly refuses to fit my world view and has embarrassed my growing belief that there is no God'. But the facts, he insists, are inescapable. 'I've become convinced of the enormous contribution that Christian evangelism makes in Africa: sharply distinct from the work of secular NGOs, government projects and international aid efforts. These alone will not do. Education and training alone will not do. In Africa Christianity changes people's hearts. It brings spiritual transformation. The rebirth is real. The change is good.'

The kingdom of God grows through evangelism as people believe the gospel that he is our saving King, and turn from sin to surrender to his rule. Of course, the kingdom will not come in its fullness until the King returns to subdue all his enemies and gather his people into his renewed creation. We are nonetheless working 'for the kingdom of God' (Colossians 4) in our evangelistic endeavours. When we pray 'Your kingdom come', we are asking for the gospel to spread throughout the world. This is our opportunity to pray for particular members of our family and friends and colleagues to become Christians and citizens of the coming kingdom! The Lord's Prayer contains this wonderful reminder to bring before God the concerns of evangelistic mission around the world.

When we pray 'Your kingdom come', we pray for the evangelization of the world, and especially of our family and friends.

We are praying for the end of the world

It is a sobering thought that, in praying 'Your kingdom come', we are asking for the end of this world. We are asking for the King to return in judgment. On the one hand, this is a marvellous thought. Our highest delight will be when our Lord finally returns to gather us into his presence. What will his face look like? How will we feel when we hear those fantastic words that will ring in our ears for ever: 'Well done, good and faithful servant'? What will his approving smile be like? What intense joy will be ours when he invites us to receive the reward he has prepared for us: 'Come, you who are blessed by my Father; take your inheritance, the kingdom prepared for you since the creation of the world' (Matthew 25:34). It's so exciting to think about seeing him, listening to him, being with him at last. What a prospect it is to be where God will 'wipe every tear from their eyes. There will be no more death or mourning or crying or pain, for the old order of things has passed away' (Revelation 21:4). We ask for all this when we pray, 'Your kingdom come'.

Yet this petition is also very sobering. We are asking for the Son of Man to reap the harvest of judgment and, in the horrific words of John, to tip the unbelievers of all nations, including our own, into 'the great winepress of God's wrath' to be crushed until their blood flows out in a lake as deep as a horse's bridle for 180 miles in all directions. This is an appalling thought. But even these images of the terrifying wrath of our Father are less horrific than Jesus' descriptions of exclusion forever in hell, which he likened to being burned alive in the furnace of God's holiness, and infested with maggots for ever. We cannot pray for this King to return to save us without also asking him to save the lost, and especially those we love. Praying 'Your kingdom come' is praying for hell as well as for heaven.

But what a victory celebration there will be when the Son 'hands over the kingdom to God the Father after he has destroyed all dominion, authority and power' (1 Corinthians 15:24)! There have been some great victory celebrations in the past: the end of the World Wars, the Olympics, World Cup celebrations, Millennium celebrations, and the Band Aid, Live Aid and Live Earth global rock concerts. I recall taking to the streets of London with thousands of joyful fans when Martin Johnson's England rugby team returned from Sydney in 2003 with the Webb Ellis World Cup trophy. What a glorious day that was, for England supporters, at least! But nothing in all of human history will compare to that epic day when the Son hands over the kingdom of God to the Father. We will talk about that moment for ever. 'Where were you in the crowd . . . did you see when he . . . did you catch the look on his face . . . wasn't the music amazing?' It is for that day that we ask when we pray to our Father, 'Your kingdom come'.

We are praying to come home

I wonder if you've seen the hugely popular American TV show *Extreme Makeover*? In this wonderfully sentimental programme, a severely disadvantaged family living in terrible conditions will have a marvellous new home built for them by the NBC television network. The family are whisked off to a theme park for a week's holiday and, while they're away, an enormous team of designers and builders, led by the celebrity presenter Ty Pennington, will destroy the old hovel and construct an immense mansion in its place. The new home will have state-of-the-art technology and glorious comforts on the grandest scale, with no expense spared. When the house is finished, the local community all gather to welcome the family home. There are tear-jerking emotional scenes as the family are shown around their fabulous new home, overcome with excitement. It's fantastic television.

One of the best things about the show is how the design team invite the local community to get involved. Local tradesmen, builders, sports teams and neighbours of every kind are encouraged to lend a hand in the thrilling transformation.

Praying 'Your kingdom come' is rather like this, but on an infinitely grander scale. Christians are invited by Jesus to get involved in God's 'Extreme Makeover' of the universe. He is creating a marvellous new home for his people. The designs were completed even before he made this world. The foundation cornerstone has already been laid in Christ crucified. The twelve foundations are named after the apostles of Christ, and the twelve gates after the tribes of Israel, signifying the presence of Old and New Testament believers. As people come to Christ each day through repentance and faith in him, they are added like 'living stones' to our Father's house, built up by the word of his grace. Jesus has gone back to heaven to finish preparing this place for each of us.

We are invited to contribute to the construction of this new home in our ministries of evangelism and serving others for Christ (1 Corinthians 3). Soon, the Father will gather his immense family into their new home for his Son's great wedding banquet (Revelation 21; 1 Peter 2; John 14). When we pray 'Your kingdom come', we tell our heavenly 'Dad' how much we long to be home with him and all the family enjoying the 'Extreme Makeover' of our Father's creation. We often feel dissatisfied in this world, frustrated with our own frailty and sin, feeling far from home like homesick strangers. But 'Your kingdom come' reminds us that our King is preparing a magnificently rebuilt home for us – the kingdom of God.

In the Lord's Prayer, Jesus teaches us to . . .

ENJOY OUR FATHER AS THE KING
. . . AS HIS LOYAL CITIZENS

So how might we pray this in practice?

'Tall skinny latte, please.' Caz was ordering coffee in Starbucks, waiting for Louisa to arrive. They'd have a good hour before Guy was due to turn up at 8pm to take her out for dinner. Caz didn't know Louisa that well but she'd just joined Caz's cell group after moving to London. Caz felt she should be friendly, so she'd offered to catch up after work. Louisa arrived in a noisy heap of bright green. She'd got a job in one of those niche graphic design companies in Covent Garden and had that flamboyance that Caz sometimes envied. They settled into comfy chairs and began to natter. The conversation with Andy had gone well. He was surprisingly sheepish about his swearing and she thought she might try a Christian book on him soon. She didn't want to scare him away by being too zealous, and certainly didn't want him to think she was chasing him. Louisa suggested something by Rico Tice and then talked, fast, about her design project. It sounded fun, but very precarious. Caz had seen girls crash and burn in graphic design before and Louisa seemed a bit naive. But Caz warmed to her as she talked of wanting to live distinctively as a citizen of heaven.

Then Louisa began to chat about her non-Christian flatmates. They sounded pretty full-on. Parties every weekend, people staying over, one actively gay girl, and they all drank shed-loads. She wanted to love them and to explain the gospel, but not to be dragged into their lifestyle. She was feeling pretty lonely and weak. Where she'd lived before was nothing like this and her parents were traditional Christians who wouldn't really understand.

Caz and Louisa talked for a bit and then Caz boldly suggested that they pray. As they hunched over their coffee mugs, Caz thought she'd try using the next phrase of the Lord's Prayer: 'Your kingdom come . . .'

'Father, we praise you that you are King and totally in control of Louisa's flat. Please establish your rule in Louisa's life; help her to live as a citizen of your coming kingdom and to remember that she's not in Satan's kingdom now . . . er . . .

'And please, Father, may your kingdom grow into the lives of these flatmates through your gospel. Give Louisa opportunities to explain that Jesus is the King and how he died to save us and help each one to accept his rule . . . er . . .

'Father, we know your kingdom's coming soon and then this world will end, so please encourage Louisa with the hope of seeing you and coming home to live with you and all your people in your paradise. Help her to keep loving her flatmates even when they're annoying, because she knows about your terrible wrath to come. Father, please rule over this and protect Louisa from harm, because you love her so much and your Son is the King. Amen.'

Louisa started to cry a bit, so Caz stopped praying and gave her a hug. She brightened up and said she was really grateful and could they meet again next week. Caz was surprised at being so helpful. The Lord's Prayer was proving useful. But, as Louisa left, Guy arrived and her stomach was suddenly sick with excitement . . .

And meanwhile . . .
Tony lay on his back and stared at his canvas sky. Sleep was difficult – it was stiflingly hot as usual. The men were restless and Davis was snoring already. He was sectioned off in the canteen, but the noise was still loud and relentless. No shelling yet, but the occasional passing trucks and APCs ruined the silence, and the moonlight was much brighter than back home. He missed Jess and the kids so much at night; she'd be putting the kids to bed about now. Tony was mulling over the day's operation and wondering how to pray. His platoon had

done well – tight and efficient. But Taylor's injury was upsetting for everyone. He'd certainly lost his left leg and the right didn't look too clever when they'd finally pulled him clear of his upturned Land Rover. The Taliban had apparently mined right up to the ridge. Tony had been in Afghanistan for five months now. He'd done several tours before and was used to the fear and the hardships. But injuries and losses were always disturbing, and he often found it hard to pray.

He'd been raised in a little Baptist church in Kent and converted at fourteen. He'd been Christian Union leader at Nottingham University and had wondered about becoming a minister. But his father and uncle had been Green Jackets before him, and the Army needs the gospel. His life's ambition was realized when he received his commission at Sandhurst from his father's great friend, Brigadier Milestone.

But how do you pray when friends are getting killed and you're dishing out death each day? Tony had always found Jesus' attitude to military men in Scripture so encouraging. The Lord seemed to understand the realities of life where many Christian friends couldn't. And Jesus' prayer had proved a godsend. When he was too exhausted or frazzled to think of anything to say or crippled by fear of an imminent operation, he'd just pray the Lord's Prayer until he fell asleep. The Father would understand.

But now he was wide awake and working through it carefully.

'Your kingdom come . . . ' Father, I praise you that you are King of kings and you rule over battles and war. Thank you for bringing me and my men back alive today. Please help Taylor to recover well and to cope with his disability.

Father, thank you for rescuing me to become a citizen in the kingdom of your Son; help me to fight bravely, knowing that if I die tomorrow I will come home to be with you and Jesus in your glorious paradise kingdom.

'Father, please comfort Jess and the girls with your sovereignty. Help Jess to teach Billy and Flo to surrender to you and trust you as King over their lives and mine. I pray that every soldier in 'K' Platoon and also my enemies will submit to you as King. Please give me a chance with each of the men, especially young Williams, who seems intrigued. Father, you know they're frightened. Help them to see that my strength comes from you.

'And, Father, this world is such a mess and this war is helping no-one. Please come back soon, King Jesus; please bring your wonderful kingdom and end this chaos and carnage. Bring peace and justice, Lord Jesus, and reign for ever, and I can't wait to meet you, Lord. Amen.'

Tony drifted off. Further up the valley, the Taliban laid some more mines.

5 'Your will be done on earth as it is in heaven . . .'

(Caring about our Father's plans)

When Jesus faced the agonies of crucifixion as he prayed in the garden of Gethsemane, just across the Kidron Valley from Jerusalem, he ended his cries to the Father with the submissive bottom line of all prayer, 'Yet not as I will, but as you will' (Matthew 26:39). In this surrender, our salvation was secured. We shall never fully understand the scale of the horror he faced. We must never underestimate how much love (for his Father and for us) it took for him to give himself up to our hell. Jesus cried out to the Father in the deepest anguish to be relieved of such a bitter 'cup' of judgment. This request to be excused the cross was not rebellious, but the righteous behaviour of a man facing unspeakable pain. But, in his prayers, he surrendered himself completely to the will of his Father whose word in Scripture had said it must be so.

The Lord's Prayer invites us to walk humbly in these holy footmarks, daily to accept God's will for our lives, however painful that path may be. Disciples of Jesus must learn to pray not that our will is done, but that our heavenly Father's will is done. As we do this, we begin to understand and share in the true holiness of our Lord Jesus Christ. We must learn to pray with the Psalmist, 'Teach me to do your will, for you are my God' (Psalm 143).

When Jesus tells his disciples to pray 'Your will be done, on earth as it is in heaven', he tells us that there are many in heaven in the presence of God who delight to do his will. There are angelic beings, his 'mighty ones who do his bidding, who obey his word' (Psalm 103). There are believers who have gone to be with the Lord, awaiting their resurrection bodies, also doing his will, for 'they are before the throne of God and serve him day and night' (Revelation 7). In the Lord's Prayer, Jesus is telling us to pray that everyone on this earth, including ourselves, will obey our Father as perfectly and as gladly as those in heaven are doing right now. So how are we to surrender to our Father's will?

It's helpful to think of two aspects of God's will: his 'secret will' and his 'revealed will'.

Our Father's 'secret will' is being done everywhere

Our Father's **secret will** is what he chooses to decree will happen, without telling us. We discover some of this will as it unfolds in the history of our planet and our lives. Each day we read newspaper reports of what God has secretly willed to happen. But most of his secret will remains hidden, for we have no idea what God has willed today for most people in the world, let alone for each molecule of every far-flung star in his countless galaxies. We can be sure, however, that everything that ever happens always happens 'according to the plan of him who works out everything in conformity with the purpose of his will' (Ephesians 1).

It is humbling to realize that our Father's will directs our lives. James rebuked the pride of his ambitious readers: 'Now listen, you who say, "Today or tomorrow we will go to this or that city, spend a year there, carry on business and make money". Why, you do not even know what will happen tomorrow. What is your life? You are a mist that appears for a little while and then vanishes.

Instead, you ought to say, "If it is the Lord's will, we will live and do this or that." As it is, you boast and brag. All such boasting is evil' (James 4:13–16). In praying 'Your will be done', we are humbled to accept that God is in control of our lives and to trust and welcome what he plans for us.

We find this particularly difficult in three major areas of life: sin, suffering and salvation.

God's secret will is not responsible for our sin

We might protest that if God's will is being done, then God is responsible for the sin people commit. But the Bible is careful to explain that God is only and always good, and never responsible for our sin. But he is able to perfectly accomplish his will and plans not only despite the sin of mankind, but through it. The obvious examples are Joseph and Jesus.

When Joseph was reunited with his wicked brothers who had sold him into slavery, he said to them, 'It was to save lives that God sent me ahead of you . . . You intended to harm me, but God intended it for good to accomplish what is now being done, the saving of many lives' (Genesis 45:5; 50:20). Joseph's brothers were completely responsible for their vindictive cruelty. But God had planned to use their evil for good. Our Father is truly amazing.

This pattern of human cruelty being used by God for good, indeed for the salvation of many, was fulfilled in the execution of Jesus. Peter told the Jewish leaders, 'This man was handed over to you by God's set purpose and foreknowledge; and you, with the help of wicked men, put him to death by nailing him to the cross. But God raised him from the dead . . . ' (Acts 2:23). Our Father's plans were not hindered, but actually accomplished, through human wickedness.

The Bible teaches both 'human responsibility' and 'divine sovereignty'. We are all responsible and guilty before God for our sin. But human wickedness, in ourselves or in others, does not thwart or delay our Father's good plans for ourselves and our world. This is a source of great reassurance for Christians.

Our Father's secret will is entirely free: God can do whatever he pleases. Those with an over-optimistic view of humanity often assert that we have 'free will'. Certainly, we make our own decisions! But the Bible attributes 'free will' to God alone, as in 'God has mercy on whom he wants to have mercy and he hardens whom he wants to harden' (Romans 9:18). We all have a 'will', but until we are freed from sin by Christ and receive his Holy Spirit, our will isn't free because we are enslaved by the ways of this world (corrupt attitudes), the prince of the air (Satan's lies) and our own sinful desires (selfish instincts) (Ephesians 2:1–3). Even after we have been reborn of the Holy Spirit, our sinful nature continues to pull us back into bondage to sinful behaviour. We make decisions unhindered, but we cannot think straight. Just as a heroin addict takes his drug 'freely' in that no-one forces him to inject himself, he is not really free but in bondage. He is responsible, but he is not free. In the same way, we are in our sinful nature addicted to sin and responsible, for no-one forces us to sin, but we can't stop because we are not free. Only God is free to will as he chooses. God is sovereign, but we are still responsible for our sin. God's secret will does not excuse our sin.

God's secret will does not delight in suffering

It is vital to recognize that God does not take equal delight in all that he decrees, for example: 'I take no pleasure in the death of anyone, declares the Sovereign Lord. Repent and live!' (Ezekiel 18:32). Our Father sustains the power of evil in this world, although he hates it. He sustains the strength of the murderer's arm and takes the life of his stabbed victim. But our Father will punish that murderer one day.

God's judgment on our rebellion against him includes the subjection of creation to futility, decay and pain. But God does not enjoy the death and destruction brought by earthquakes and tsunamis upon the earth. Indeed, he has done something magnificent and costly to redeem his world and his people from evil and suffering.

Our Father wills suffering for a greater good

People often say that if God is both good and powerful then he must end suffering, and that, since he doesn't, he can't exist. But they forget the other possibility. God's secret will decrees that terrible things must continue to happen to achieve a good that is greater than the evil of suffering: the salvation of many: 'The Lord is not slow in keeping his promise, as some understand slowness. He is patient with you, not wanting anyone to perish, but everyone to come to repentance. But the day of the Lord will come like a thief' (2 Peter 3:9–10). Only God can know when 'enough is enough'.

In the midst of suffering, we don't need pious platitudes or theological debate, but someone to listen and cry with us. However, to prepare for suffering and to pray the Lord's Prayer in the midst of it, we must understand why our loving Father wills suffering. The Bible does not avoid these questions, but teaches a great deal about them because we worship the Suffering Servant. The escapism of Buddhism, the fatalism of Hinduism and the submission of Islam compare very poorly.

It's helpful to consider four statements that summarize the Bible's perspective.

We have all contributed to bringing suffering upon ourselves

Our human rebellion against God has brought suffering into this world. The original rebellion of our representative ancestors, Adam and Eve, has excluded us all from the paradise garden. But we would have behaved just as they did. We are therefore all caught in the vortex of decay and death imposed by God on this world because of human sin. Cancer, car accidents and coffins all originate in human defiance of our Creator, a defiance that is undiminished in human hearts today.

Suffering is sometimes directly caused by sin. The brutality of war and ethnic cleansing are plainly from mankind and not God. The death camps of Hitler, Stalin and Pol Pot should crush our confidence in man rather than God. The reason that an earthquake in California kills two people but in India kills 20,000 is the unequal distribution of wealth expressed in different qualities of housing. Global warming and famine are caused by human greed and ecological irresponsibility. Terrorism is committed by religious fanatics and not by God. Indeed, the sad but brutal fact is that, like many diseases, Aids is spreading because of immorality, and orphaned children suffer for it. Our Father derives no joy from the pain we have brought upon ourselves and is clearly committed to saving as many as will trust in his Son for a new world without suffering. But our Father's secret will is not responsible for the sin that has brought this suffering upon us. We are.

It is important to emphasize that Jesus explicitly rejects the notion that suffering can be confidently attributed to judgment for particular sins. Although liver failure can be the direct result of alcoholism, the tower in Siloam, that fell and killed eighteen people in Jesus' day, did not fall on those who were more guilty than others (Luke 13:1–5). Unlike the Muslim clerics who attributed the appalling loss of life caused by the Boxing Day tsunami in South-East Asia to decadent lifestyle, Jesus discouraged speculation about links between sin and tragedy. But he did say that something much worse is coming. The judgment of the Son of Man will be more horrific than any tsunami, and we must warn everyone who will listen. On that day God will certainly punish specific sins as the gospel declares (Romans 2:16).

God has joined us in our suffering
God has not remained aloof, but took flesh in Jesus to help us. Christ did not come as a prince in a palace or a philosopher in

a university. As a child, he was a hunted refugee; as an adult, a tradesman in a poor province of an occupied territory; in his ministry, poor, homeless and hated by the establishment; in the end he was betrayed and deserted by his followers, unjustly tried and condemned, brutally tortured and cruelly killed.

God offered his Son, and his Son volunteered for such suffering, so that we might enjoy his grace for ever. We cannot accuse God of ignoring our suffering. He has joined us in suffering to deliver us from it – because he loves us. Christians derive great comfort from praying to our Father, who understands our pain because he has sacrificed his beloved Son to incredible suffering for us.

Christ has opened a costly way into a pain-free world

No-one can accuse God of doing nothing about the suffering in the world. Christ suffered our death to rise as the firstborn from the dead to launch the new age of resurrection and to open the way into his renewed creation. There God himself will dwell with us. 'He will wipe every tear from their eyes. There will be no more death or mourning or crying or pain, for the old order of things has passed away. He who was seated on the throne said, "I am making everything new"' (Revelation 21:4–5).

Hearing news, as I write, of a Christian killed in a car accident, leaving a terribly injured wife and two young children without a father, at least they can know that Jesus died so that they can be reunited with their dad in heaven one day, when all their tears will be tenderly wiped away for ever. What a joyful reunion that will be.

Our Father can bring good out of our suffering

God graciously alleviates our hardships with countless good gifts and can even bring good out of our suffering.

We learn moral awareness from experiencing the consequences of sin. We also learn to empathize and care for others through our own suffering. Those who've been through pain and grief are usually better able to care for others.

C. S. Lewis, who nursed his wife as she died of cancer, observed that we are more open to God in suffering than we are in comfort. In *The Problem of Pain*, he famously observed, 'God whispers in our pleasures, speaks in our conscience but shouts in our pains. It is his megaphone to rouse a deaf world.'[1] Indeed, down the ages and across the world, suffering has been a reason for seeking God rather than hating him. Modern Westerners see suffering as a barrier to belief in God because they've acquired a false image of a God who could not allow pain to continue.

Furthermore, Christians learn in suffering to become like Christ, for, 'in all things God works for the good of those who love him, who have been called according to his purpose. For those God foreknew he also predestined to be conformed to the likeness of his Son' (Romans 8:28–29). Suffering is a school for Christians, though 'it is better, if it is God's will, to suffer for doing good than for doing evil' (1 Peter 3:17). God's family are not immune from the suffering of this world (or we would be believers for purely personal benefit rather than out of loving faith in God). We must also face the additional pain of persecution for Christ. Prayer only rarely heals pain, for our Father usually prefers to send other members of his family to support us through it so that they and we can become more like Jesus. Praying 'Your will be done' reminds us that it is God's will and not Satan's will or fate that is being done. In this we can be content, because we know our Father loves and wants the best for us. God's secret will takes no delight in our suffering, but uses it for our good in becoming like Jesus.

Our Father's secret will includes personal salvation

God's choosing or 'electing' his people before creation and 'predestining' us for heaven is simply the individual aspect of his sovereign will directing all things. Many struggle to understand, and some intensely dislike, this doctrine, but it is certainly taught by the apostles and by Jesus. Paul says that God 'chose us in him before the creation of the world to be holy and blameless in his sight. In love he predestined us to be adopted as his sons through Jesus Christ, in accordance with his pleasure and will . . . In him we were also chosen, having been predestined according to the plan of him who works out everything in conformity with the purpose of his will' (Ephesians 1:4–5, 11).

Jesus also taught that he had come to save those who had been given to him by the Father, known as the 'elect'. He said, 'For I have come down from heaven not to do my will but to do the will of him who sent me. And this is the will of him who sent me, that I shall lose none of all that he has given me, but raise them up at the last day' (John 6:38–39). This truth is given by God, not to trouble us with pointless speculations about who might be chosen, but to comfort the people of God with the knowledge that Christ will not lose any of his chosen people. When we pray 'Your will be done', we surrender to God's electing will. For ourselves, we can rejoice that, as we have become Christians, the Father's will is that Christ will never lose us, but raise us up on the last day. For others whom we long to be saved, we both surrender to God's election (in the knowledge that if God did not elect people then no-one has any hope of salvation) and rejoice that God seems to delight in electing and saving those for whom we pray. Praying 'Your will be done' reminds us that, however proud and cynical people are, God may yet have other plans for them in his secret will!

When we pray 'Your will be done', we submit ourselves and our families and our world to our Father's secret decrees, trusting that his will is always good and just, even though we don't know much of it yet. When my nephew was on a life-support machine for weeks in Guy's Hospital in London, it was a great comfort to my Christian brother and his wife that our Father's secret will is always done. They could trust that whatever God willed for their little boy was good, even if it meant his death. They took the view that our Father could either heal their son in the hospital, or heal him in the new creation. Either way, their little boy was safe in our Father's good and secret will. Sadly, unbelievers have no such reassurance.

Simply put, we can say to our Father, 'Your will be done', because we trust that he is utterly good.

From our Father's secret will, we now turn to consider his 'revealed will', published in Scripture, for 'The secret things belong to the LORD our God, but the things revealed belong to us and to our children for ever, that we may follow all the words of this law' (Deuteronomy 29:29)

Our Father's 'revealed will' is found in Scripture

Contrary to the belief that God neither knows nor plans the future, our Father is weaving his plans skilfully together to accomplish the part of his will that he has revealed in Scripture: 'What I have said, that will I bring about; what I have planned, that will I do' (Isaiah 46:11).

We can pray in confidence for the things that our Father has said he wants to do in our lives and in our world. J. I. Packer writes perceptively:

> His range of revealed purpose as he deals with this fallen world includes the producing of what is morally, spiritually, aesthetically and culturally good; making unbelievers godly through redemption, regeneration, sanctification and glorification; advancing the kingdom of Christ worldwide; gathering and building up the one church of Christ in every place; maturing, enriching, and perfecting his adopted children in their relationship with himself; exposing and punishing evil; displaying the glory of his holy love, wisdom, truth and justice and of his unlimited cosmic and trans-cosmic powers and eliciting praise for it all from angels and humans alike. All the specific acts of God in his sovereign ordering of world events and individual lives are means,

one way or another, to the furthering of this array of ends, and into this frame of purposive divine action our petitionary prayers should fit, for they too, in some way that is beyond our full understanding, will also be means towards these ends.[2]

The plans and will of God, published in Scripture, remain the will of our Father, and never date or become irrelevant. 'The plans of the LORD stand firm for ever, the purposes of his heart through all generations' (Psalm 33:11).

Our Father's revealed will is to put everything under Christ

Our Father has clearly published his general plan for our world: 'And he made known to us the mystery of his will according to his good pleasure, which he purposed in Christ, to be put into effect when the times will have reached their fulfilment – to bring all things in heaven and on earth together under one head, even Christ' (Ephesians 1:9–10). When we pray, 'Your will be done' we are asking our Father to fulfil this marvellous plan to bring everything together under Christ.

Our specific role in this plan is to submit ourselves willingly to the headship of Christ so that 'through the church, the manifold wisdom of God should be made known to the rulers and authorities in the heavenly realms, according to his eternal purpose which he accomplished in Christ Jesus our Lord' (Ephesians 3:10). The reconciliation of the church to God, and to each other, in holy love and unity of faith, declares for all the world to see the eternal purpose of our Father to bring everything under Christ.

Our Father's revealed will is to make us like Christ

When Paul famously explained that 'in all things God works for the good of those who love him, who have been called according to his purpose', he goes on to explain his purpose for us: 'to be conformed to the likeness of his Son' (Romans 8:28–29). Various passages spell out what God's will means for us in practice.

Self-sacrificial worship is God's will for our lives: 'Therefore, I urge you, brothers, in view of God's mercy, to offer your bodies as living sacrifices, holy and pleasing to God – this is your spiritual act of worship. Do not conform any longer to the pattern of this world, but be transformed by the renewing of your mind. Then you will be able to test and approve what God's will is – his good, pleasing and perfect will' (Romans 12:1–2). Self-sacrificial service, adoration and submission to God in worship help us to recognize what God's will is for us in any given situation.

Evangelism is God's will for our lives. 'Be very careful, then, how you live – not as unwise but as wise, making the most of every opportunity, because the days are evil. Therefore do not be foolish, but understand what the Lord's will is. Do not get drunk on wine, which leads to debauchery. Instead, be filled with the Spirit' (Ephesians 5:15–18). Wise and opportunistic evangelistic holiness, empowered by the Holy Spirit, is God's will for us.

Holiness is God's will for our lives: 'It is God's will that you should be sanctified: that you should avoid sexual immorality' (1 Thessalonians 4:3). Like a chauffeur steering a priceless Bentley well clear of the parked cars, we are to keep ourselves clear of situations in which we are likely to crash into immorality. Whenever we place a limit on our alcohol intake, install a barrier to porn on our laptops, decline an invitation to socialize with a married colleague or to visit a strip bar after work, or refuse to entertain a girlfriend or boyfriend in our bedroom or alone on holiday, we are accepting God's will for our lives. And our Father loves it.

Contentedness is God's will for our lives. 'Give thanks in all circumstances, for this is God's will for you in Christ Jesus' (1 Thessalonians 5:18). In an ungrateful and complaining culture obsessed with acquisition and self-satisfaction, the secret of contentedness in need and in plenty, accepting the will of God, is to recognize 'I can do everything through him who gives me strength' (Philippians 4:13). Confident that God will always supply what we need, we can remain thankful in all circumstances and follow the will of our Father.

In these and other ways, we demonstrate that we are God's children by our willingness to become like the Son. Jesus said, 'Whoever does the will of my Father in heaven is my brother and sister and mother' (Matthew 12:50).

Our Father's revealed will is found in Scripture and not in 'signs'
The Bible celebrates the guidance of God. He leads us through life like a shepherd and we hear his voice in the Scriptures (Psalm 23; John 10). When the book of Hebrews quotes from the Old Testament, it says 'God says' or 'the Holy Spirit says' in the present tense. The Bible contains the words of the Holy Spirit speaking today. Just as our breath carries our words out of our mouths when we speak, the breath (Spirit) of God carries forth his Word (Scripture) about the full and final Word from God, Jesus Christ our Lord.

Many Christians are confused about this. Many who long to obey God's will suffer under the expectation that our Father is trying, with only modest success, to steer us into his personal 'will' for our lives. They fear missing his will for their blessing and are burdened with theories about how to discern God's leading and hear his voice today. By way of illustration, consider the following letter from an anxious young Christian.

Dear Pastor Jack,

STRICTLY PRIVATE AND CONFIDENTIAL

Please can you help me? I'm anxious to discern God's will for my life as I decide whether to apply to Aberdeen or Cardiff University. My parents now live in Edinburgh so I wonder if God wants me to honour them by

*going to Aberdeen, or to love my brother who lives near Cardiff by going
there. My boyfriend is at Bristol University studying medicine, so I'm not
sure if God wants me to be near him so we can see each other more and
perhaps get married or to put God first and go to Glasgow. I love skiing
and would love to join a university club, which I could do in Aberdeen,
but it may be that God wants me to make the sacrifice for him and go to
Cardiff. The Christian Union in Cardiff is apparently stronger than at
Aberdeen, but I don't know if God is telling me to go to Cardiff for better
teaching or to Glasgow to serve more?*

*My friends think that Aberdeen has the better night life – but is that
from the devil? I'm trying to be open to God's signs but can you tell me
how many signs should point to the same thing for me to know it's from
God? I'm very confused and need your guidance about God's guidance.
How do I find God's will for my life?*

Yours

Jenny

*PS I seem to have lost the application form for Cardiff – is that God
telling me to go to Aberdeen?*

When Jesus tells us to pray to our Father 'Your will be done, on
earth as it is in heaven', how does Jenny know his will?

The Psalmist says, 'Your word is a lamp to my feet and a light
for my path' (Psalm 119:105). Peter clarifies that there are not
many lights to live by, but one: 'We have the word of the prophets
made more certain, and you will do well to pay attention to it,
as to a light shining in a dark place, until the day dawns and the
morning star rises in your hearts' (2 Peter 1:19). In heaven, all will
be crystal clear and as bright as day and we will put our Bibles
aside. Until then, we need the lamp of Scripture or we will be
walking in darkness like Jenny.

This one light is everything we need to know from God, for
it makes us 'thoroughly equipped for every good work' (2 Timothy

3:17). There is no good work that we could want to do for God for which the Bible doesn't thoroughly equip us!

This means that, although our Father could send an angel or a vision with a special message from him, he doesn't generally do so because everything we need to know is in the Scriptures. Our usual problem is that we don't know where to look, or whom to ask for help. Special messages from angels would be a lot less helpful than a Bible with a thousand pages of living instruction for us because we can keep it by our beds and study it every day. The guidance that Jenny needs is in her Bible, whether in general principles of godliness (e.g. honouring parents, avoiding immorality, needing teaching and being willing to serve, etc.) or in the principles of the wisdom literature, fulfilled in Christ in whom all the treasures of wisdom and knowledge are hidden (e.g. 'physical training is of some value, but godliness has value for all things, holding promise for both the present life and the life to come' [1 Timothy 4:8]). If there is nothing in Scripture that determines a decision, Jenny is free to choose what she prefers and enjoy this freedom of conscience.

I once heard a recording of the great Dr Martyn Lloyd-Jones talking about hearing God's guidance from Scripture, the inner promptings of the Holy Spirit, the godly counsel of friends and sanctified common sense. I found myself wondering how you know if a prompting is from the Holy Spirit or the devil, if it is godly advice or godless advice, sanctified or sinful sense, and then it dawned on me. These are not alternative sources of guidance but alternative sources of Scripture. I could hear the voice of God in Scripture by reading it, or recalling it with the Spirit's help, or hearing it from friends or by working it out from what I know. The Bible is the guidance that Jenny and we need to know about. The Bible is our Father's revealed will for our lives.

Our Father's secret and revealed wills are perfectly complementary
In practice, the 'secret will' and the 'revealed will' of our Father perfectly complement each other. Imagine that Jenny is delayed

in her journey to her interview at Cardiff and, after fretting on the platform, eventually boards a train to find a girl alone in the carriage weeping. When Jenny asks her if she is alright, the girl asks if Jenny knows of any way to be forgiven! Jenny explains the way of salvation and leads her to the Lord Jesus. When she gets off the train she rings her friends and says, 'God led me to board a later train.'

Of course she's right. But it was God's secret will that arranged for her to be on the later train, not his revealed will. Jenny didn't hear a voice or meet an angel or have a vision. God's secret will arranged all the circumstances of her day to ensure the two girls met, and his revealed will in Scripture told her what to say about Jesus. God was leading her by both his secret will that arranges the circumstance of our lives and his revealed will which tells us how to serve him. In making decisions, we need to trust his secret will and obey his revealed will with prayerful wisdom.

'Your will be done' means surrendering our lives

In the Lord's Prayer, Jesus tells us to pray that our Father's will be done, which means, as the great Westminster Confession theologians put it, ' . . . We pray that God, by his grace, would make us willing to know, obey and submit to his will in all things . . . ' (Westminster Shorter Catechism).

One of the finest examples of surrender to the will of God is Eric Liddell, the 'Flying Scotsman' of *Chariots of Fire* fame. He played international rugby for Scotland but is more famous for his sprinting. He won national championships in both 100m and 200m in 1921, 1922, and 1923, and then, in 1924 in Paris, the Olympic 400m gold medal. But he is most admired for three extraordinary decisions that reflected the priorities of a deep surrender to our Father's will.

The first was his bold decision not to run in his preferred 100m race at the Olympics, because the heats were to be run on a

Sunday, and it was his settled conviction that Sunday should be kept special for the Lord. He pulled out of the sprint relays for the same reason and was accused of being a traitor to his country for refusing to compromise his principles. As Harold Abrahams (whom he'd earlier beaten) went on to win the gold, Eric was preaching in a church in Paris. Imagine sacrificing an Olympic medal you've trained so hard to win, for a biblical principle. This was surrender to what he believed was the revealed will of God in Scripture.

Winning the gold in his weaker event of 400m in a world-record time won him universal respect, and his second bold decision soon followed. As an Olympic celebrity, the world lay at his feet. But after the Paris Olympics, Eric Liddell enrolled at Bible college in Edinburgh and then announced that he was going to Tientsin (now Tianjin) in China, as a missionary for Christ, at the age of 23. This showed his surrender to the will of God that we make disciples of all nations.

Ordained in 1932, married in 1933, and soon with three daughters, he made a third bold decision in 1937. With the full support of his wife, but despite severe criticism from many, he responded to the desperate pleas for help from missionaries in the war-torn region of Siaochang and began leaving his family for long periods to help with gospel work in the countryside. In 1942 he was trapped by the oncoming Japanese armies and bundled off with other Europeans to the prison compound of Weihsien. There, separated from his family, he dedicated himself to the welfare of others before dying of a brain tumour in 1945. He'd shown wonderful sacrificial love. All of Scotland mourned this man who cared more for God's glory than his own and gave up everything this world offers for the salvation of others. The guiding principle of his life and the last word on his lips as he died was 'surrender'. Not passive inactivity but submission to God's will.

At his funeral, the vicar said, 'Absolute surrender to the will of God. Absolute surrender – those words were often on his lips, the concept was always in his mind; that God should have absolute control over every part of his life. It was towards the attainment of that ideal that he directed all his mental and spiritual energies.' This is what praying 'Your will be done' will mean.

In the third petition of the Lord's Prayer, Jesus tells us to

ENJOY OUR FATHER AS OUR SOVEREIGN GUIDE . . .
. . . AS HIS OBEDIENT SERVANTS

So how might we pray this in practice?

Guy brought Caz flowers – her favourite white lilies. And then they wandered along Oxford Street to eat in St Christopher's Place in a lovely little Turkish restaurant. He was being utterly charming and Caz was feeling excited and flustered at the same time. She could feel the pace picking up and was being swept along. She was normally so measured, but Guy was great fun and so kind. She was already wondering if this was permanent. She loved the fact that he talked openly about making his life count for Christ. He did talk a lot, like most men, about his plans. But they were godly plans. He was wondering about mission work abroad. What did she think? This was scary. They'd been going out for ten months, but it still felt dizzily quick to Caz.

Then she went and did it again. She suggested they pray, right there in the restaurant! She explained to Guy how she was working through the Lord's Prayer as they'd learnt to at Refresh, and Guy said he'd been using it too – a total revelation to him. But what would the

Muslim waiters think? Caz said they shouldn't mind, and bowed her head to pray. Guy smiled a mile wide and took hold of her hands as she prayed:

'*Our Father . . . your will be done* . . . Father, we praise you that you are in charge and working out your will to bring everything under the headship of Christ and for saving us as part of your plan . . . er . . .

'We praise you that your secret will is unfolding all around us and even though we don't know many of the details, we do trust that everything is working for your glory and to make us become like Christ, so please help Guy not to worry about the future. May your will be done even if that means going abroad, and make us (I mean him) willing to trust you . . .

. . . er . . .

'Help us to remember that we are still responsible for our sin. Help us not to rebel when life is hard and help us to take comfort in your will to elect us for salvation for the praise of your grace . . .

'And . . . er . . .

'We also praise you for your will revealed in Scripture, Father. Please help us to obey your written instructions for our lives and to encourage each other to live surrendered lives of worship and evangelism and holiness and contentedness – help us to be godly together.'

Suddenly it felt as if she was saying too much. She felt very embarrassed, and finished quickly, 'Sorry, Father. Amen.'

Guy asked why she'd said sorry and Caz explained sheepishly that she'd suddenly felt such a fraud praying in public when she'd never really done much praying before, and now she was doing it all day long. And that she'd said too much and was becoming a weirdo. Guy just said he thought she was fantastic. And then they walked, for hours, round Hyde Park and it was electric, and Caz had never felt so excited and frightened before. And now she felt the need to talk to the Father in heaven more than ever . . .

And meanwhile . . .
Peter sat at the dinner table trying to maintain control of three kids all trying to leave the room. 'Come on, guys,' he said, trying to sound firm but reasonable, 'we all agreed to work our way through the Lord's Prayer, phrase by phrase, and we're making good progress.'

'But that was when I didn't have homework and now I do – a giant science project in by the end of the week, Dad – you have no idea how strict Miss Collins is and this is course work that affects my whole future. You do want me to get some GCSEs, don't you? I just don't have time for this now.'

Kate always knew how to get under his skin. His wife, Julia, dived in.

'We're only doing one phrase of the Lord's Prayer – and we can pray about your project as well if you like.'

The two boys just watched with amusement. This could go either way – big screaming bust-up or Dad might just pull it off – definitely best to stay quiet when the argument was about 'Bible-time'. So they pushed back their chairs noisily and buried their heads in their arms to enjoy the fight.

'*Please*, Kate,' said her father in his sweetest voice. His daughter had a will of iron. 'I know it's not easy, so I promise I won't be long – just a few minutes.'

'But you always say that and it always last ages,' she wailed. But she did sit down again, grumpily.

Julia seized the moment and grabbed the family Bibles, notebooks and pens and dished them out quickly. She secretly signalled to Peter to get a move on. He read the Lord's Prayer and then turned to the Refresh booklet and read Ephesians 1:11 about God's will and predestination. Ben raised his ten-year-old freckles from the table. 'I don't understand perdensternation,' he said. Rob knew this was his opportunity. 'Yeah, how can we be predestinated if we have to become Christians?' he smirked at Kate.

She erupted 'You're deliberately asking that to keep us here for ever.'

'Maybe I am, maybe I'm not,' said Rob. 'It's all the will of God.'

'Right stop, everybody,' said Peter, intervening quickly. 'I'm going to pray myself tonight – now tell me what you're worried about.'

The usual litany of injuries, matches and homework followed.

So he prayed, briefly, 'Our Father . . . Your will be done . . .

We praise you that you are carrying out your plans for the whole world to save people of all nations and bring them together under Jesus Christ.

We praise you for carrying out your secret will in the world and trust you to look after all the homework and match results and cuts we all have and especially Kate's science project. Especially we thank you for choosing us to be your children for ever; we also thank you for your revealed will in Scripture. We're sorry that we so often ignore it. May your will be done in our lives as a family. Help us to learn to be kind and forgiving and patient as you want us to be. Please, if it's your will, protect Uncle Tony and help Aunty Caz make a wise decision and help

Mum and me to work out from Scripture what kind of summer holiday is within your will, in Jesus' precious name, Amen.'

Kate fled to her bedroom. Rob fled to the TV room. But Ben stayed behind. 'I'm worried about my assembly tomorrow, could we pray about that too?'

Peter threw a puzzled look in Julia's direction. 'Sure, what's happening?' He'd never asked for prayer before, but the Lord's Prayer was touching their lives in unexpected ways.

6 'Give us today our daily bread . . . '

(Needing our Father's provision)

A Christian organization recently sent me an advertisement for 'The Seven Great Prayers for Powerful Praying'. Here's a taste of what it contained:

> So here's the fourth prayer that will start ATTRACTING incredible blessings into your life – Health, Love, Money, Happiness, Purpose, a Better Relationship with God, are all yours when you pray . . . 'I ATTRACT GOD'S BLESSINGS'. Here are some variations. These variations use two of the most powerful words in the English language, I AM. When Moses saw the burning bush, he asked, 'Who are you?' And the answer Moses received was – 'I AM'. Tap into the power of God and preface your prayer requests with these two POWERFUL words: 'I AM ATTRACTING GOD'S BLESSINGS'; 'I AM HAPPY'; 'I AM FULL OF LIFE, LOVE, AND HAPPINESS'; 'I AM HEALED'; 'I AM DEBT-FREE'; 'I HAVE A GREAT JOB'. **Even if you're not any of the above, say and pray them anyway. As they say in acting school, 'Fake it until you make it'.**

The order form for the new prayer book then reads:

> Start attracting miracles and blessings into your life with this
> amazing new book. See why so many people are saying this is the
> most powerful book on prayer ever written . . . Featuring The
> Seven Great Prayers and 100 of the most POWERFUL prayers
> ever attracting HEALTH, WEALTH, HAPPINESS, BLESSINGS
> and a CLOSER RELATIONSHIP to God.

I confess that I find this utterly revolting. Prayer, we are told, is
a way of 'attracting' God's blessings like iron filings to a magnet,
rather than a means of humbly asking our heavenly Father for
help. Prayer is about using 'powerful' words such as God's holy
name to 'tap' into his power and acquire material luxuries. These
are pagan incantations, not the heartfelt pleas of children to
their Father. This advertisement treats God like a slot machine:
push the right buttons, pull the handle, and wait for the avalanche
of blessings. Such promises dishonour God and exploit Christians.

In the Lord's Prayer, Jesus teaches a completely different
attitude.

Prayer is depending upon our Father

The first three petitions have expressed our primary commitment
to our Father's reputation, rule and plans as our Lord. The second
three petitions express our humble reliance on him as our Saviour.
We depend upon our Father for his provision (of bread), pardon
(of sins) and protection (from evil).

Jesus reveals our top three personal needs

Some of our most desperate cries for help don't make it into
Jesus' top three. An ideal partner, a perfect body shape and a

dream house aren't mentioned. Jesus wants us to think bigger and more long-term. He wants us to learn new priorities concerned with eternal life in him. He wants us to ask for the provision of 'bread' to preserve us from death, the pardon of 'debts' to preserve us from sin, and deliverance from 'evil' to protect us from Satan.

It's striking that Jesus doesn't articulate massive global issues. He was well aware of the evils of slavery, leprosy and Roman occupation in his own day, as we are aware today of climate change, poverty, Aids and terrorism. Yet he focuses here on our personal needs.

Of course, these petitions can certainly include the big issues that reappear in every generation. We can pray about climate change and poverty when we ask for daily bread; we can pray about Aids and abortion when we ask for pardon for our sins; we can pray about terrorism and war when we ask for protection from evil. But remembering Jesus' personal language may keep us from becoming too grand and theoretical in our prayers. It's sometimes tempting to worry and campaign about global issues while neglecting people's personal need for our heavenly Father.

It is amazing how simple and yet comprehensive these three brilliant little phrases are. They summarize our deepest personal needs.

We ask our Father to *provide* daily bread

One of God's names is 'Jahweh-Jireh' (Lord-Provider), which reminds us that we need to rely on him every day. God is at work not only in the unusual and the spectacular. He also constantly provides for our ordinary everyday needs in our homes, in the shops, in public services and in the places where we work.

We ask our Father for *daily bread*

The word Jesus used for 'bread' is the ordinary word for ordinary bread. It's commonly used in the Bible to signify basic human needs: food, warmth, clothing, a home.

The word for 'daily' is, however, notoriously difficult to translate. It means 'for the coming day', which could mean 'for today' or 'for tomorrow', or any number of slight variations. There is also some debate about the precise nature of the 'daily bread' we are to pray for. Some say it refers solely to spiritual nourishment, while others limit it to physical provision. I don't think we need to be so restrictive. Jesus deliberately chose a word with a broad meaning to encompass the whole range of human needs.

This becomes clear if we consider the biblical background to this petition – God's provision of bread for Israel during their journey to the Promised Land. This epic experience taught so many important lessons about God's providential care that a portion of the bread provided by God was permanently kept in a gold jar in the tabernacle.

Let's consider three of these lessons, and reflect on how Jesus applied them in his teaching.

'Daily bread' includes our physical needs
Israel had to learn to trust God to provide them with food to survive their journey. When Israel escaped from slavery in Egypt and cried out for food, the Lord said, 'I will rain down bread from heaven for you' (Exodus 16:4). When the Israelites collected this bread, or 'manna' (lit., 'what is it?'), they found it was flakes like wafers made with honey (like Frosties® cereal). Every day for forty years God provided enough to feed everyone.

In the same way, our loving Father delights to provide for our practical needs. He is our Creator and Sustainer and he draws us close to himself by feeding us each day. We should never imagine that such things are unimportant to our Father. 'Every good and perfect gift is from above' (James 1:17). Behind the countless joys of life is our smiling Father, raining down his blessings on us each and every day. We must learn to ask for them and trust him to provide these material needs.

God gave Israel instructions to test whether they could learn to obey him. He told them to collect only enough manna for each day. But they disobeyed and gathered too much, and the excess manna became infested with maggots. Again, God told them to collect twice as much on Fridays, so they wouldn't need to work on the Sabbath (Saturday). But again they disobeyed and went out to collect more manna on Saturdays, but this time there was none to be found. God was training his people to be satisfied with what he gave them, and to accept his bountiful gifts obediently, in accordance with his Word.

Indeed, this lesson was later explained by Moses: 'Man does not live on bread alone but on every word that comes from the mouth of the LORD' (Deuteronomy 8:3). It was not simply the manna that kept them alive; God's Word provided the bread and sustained them on their long journey. Like Adam and Eve before them, they failed to realize that God's gifts must be received in obedience to his Word.

Thankfully, Jesus, our Saviour and representative, knew better. When Satan tempted Jesus to get himself some bread when he was hungry in the desert (Matthew 4), he quoted Moses' words to Satan! As the head of a new humanity and founder of a new people of God, he refused to disobey the Father by submitting to the devil. He resisted temptation where Adam and Israel had failed.

Like Jesus, we need to trust our Father to provide for our needs. We should not become anxious or disobey his commands in an effort to acquire more than he gives us. It is not nature, but our Father's Word using nature and technology, that sustains us every day.

In times of hardship, we would do well to remember that, before he fed Israel, God humbled them by letting them go hungry. The Lord was teaching them to depend on him, disciplining them through hardship as a loving Father: 'As a man disciplines his son, so the Lord your God disciplines you.' Difficult times of material shortage, such as recession and redundancy, painful though they may be, are also opportunities for us to grow in conscious dependence on God, and times of training for the children he loves.

Moses explained that God taught Israel to depend on him in this way in order to help them remain faithful in times of prosperity: 'You may say to yourself, "My power and the strength of my hands have produced this wealth for me",' Moses warned. 'But remember the LORD your God, for it is he who gives you the ability to produce wealth' (Deuteronomy 8:17–18). We too need to learn these lessons in the hard times so that we won't forget God when life is comfortable and prosperous.

A wealthy Christian businessman I know had been generous in supporting gospel work, but then lost a fortune in the scandalous collapse of the energy company ENRON. He showed me around the empty ENRON building where he had worked. The vast and lifeless shell of a financial empire reminded me of some kind of sunken shipwreck. He was surprisingly calm about his financial losses. 'I have repeatedly acknowledged to God that my wealth comes from him,' he said. 'I've asked that, if at any point he thought it would be spiritually better for me not to have it, he would please take it away. I trust that this is what he has done and I am content with that.' This man had learned the lesson of the manna.

In our godless nation, where many people are wealthier than ever before, few seem to have turned to God in gratitude. Though none of us welcome times of painful economic downturn, perhaps they may call some away from trusting in wealth to trust in God. Jesus tells us to ask for 'daily bread' to remind us of our daily dependence on our Father and so to ask him for our material needs.

'Daily bread' includes our spiritual needs
Jesus taught that God's provision of manna for Israel is fulfilled not only in our Father's granting of material resources, but also

in his providing for our spiritual needs. John's Gospel records how Jesus fed a very large crowd from a boy's bread rolls and fish, before explaining, 'I am the living bread that came down from heaven. If anyone eats of this bread, he will live for ever. This bread is my flesh, which I will give for the life of the world' (John 6:51). Jesus plainly saw his crucified body as the essential 'bread' to sustain and nourish our spiritual life. Jesus saw himself as God's bread 'from heaven', the fulfilment of the manna in the desert.

Christians everywhere continue to remember the broken body of Jesus on the cross in Holy Communion or the Lord's Supper. Some may wonder whether the petition for 'daily bread' in the Lord's Prayer is related to his teaching at the Last Supper, Jesus' final Passover meal, when he 'took bread, gave thanks and broke it . . . saying, "Take and eat; this is my body"' (Matthew 26). The bread broken at the Passover meal does not primarily recall the manna in the desert, but the unleavened bread of the Passover feast. Originally eaten in haste by the Israelites before they left Egypt, this was never intended to be 'daily bread', but rather an annual celebration. When we pray 'Give us today our daily bread', we are therefore not asking for daily Holy Communion.

However, the unleavened bread of the Passover and the manna of the wilderness are related, for both are fulfilled in Jesus. The unleavened bread, recalled in the Lord's Supper, symbolized the separation of Israel from the ungodliness of Egypt (unleavened because the yeast had been 'separated' from the dough). Together with the sacrificed lamb, it marked the deliverance of Israel from captivity at the start of their journey. The manna, on the other hand, was provided to keep the people going after their journey had begun. By fulfilling both the manna and the unleavened bread through his death on the cross, Jesus both sets us on the way to our Promised Land and keeps us going throughout the journey. He claimed to fulfil the lamb and unleavened bread at the Passover meal in the upper room, and also to be the manna from heaven at the feeding of the 5,000. In both cases, he teaches that it is his broken, crucified body that sustains our journey to heaven. The Lord's Supper reminds us that his crucifixion delivered us from bondage. The Lord's Prayer reminds us that his crucified body continues to sustain us on our journey to the promised kingdom of God.

When we share the Lord's Supper and when we pray the Lord's Prayer, we are intended to feed upon our crucified Saviour by faith, personally trusting his sacrifice to save us and taking him deep into our souls to nourish our confidence in him.

'Daily bread' includes our future needs

We have already seen that the Israelites were told to gather twice as much manna as usual on the day before the Sabbath. On these occasions the extra manna did not decay or become infested with maggots, as it would have done on other days. This was necessary because God sent no manna on the Sabbath. He wanted his people to do no ordinary work on that day, for the Sabbath symbolized the 'rest', the secure peace with God, for which they and we were created and then redeemed (Exodus 20; Deuteronomy 5).

The Sabbath rest enjoyed by the Israelites in the wilderness symbolizes the 'rest' that awaits us: life in Christ in the new creation. Just as God promised to provide bread for the Israelites' Sabbath rest, so also he promises to provide for our future in his kingdom. We pray for this when we pray for 'daily bread' in the Lord's Prayer. We are asking God's provision not only for today, but for the eternal rest to come in heaven.

The Israelites experienced a partial fulfilment of their Sabbath rest when they arrived in the Promised Land. The manna which had sustained them for forty years stopped on that day, but that did not mark the end of God's provision. On the contrary, God continued to bless them more bountifully than ever before, as they began to eat of the rich produce of Canaan. What the manna of the Sabbath had symbolized, they now fully enjoyed in God's provision of rich food supplies in the Promised Land.

In a similar way, the life to which we look forward in the new creation is immeasurably greater than anything we now experience. Jesus' crucified body, our broken bread, sustains us throughout our lives until we cross through death into the new creation. But God's provision does not then come to an end; rather, it reaches its fulfilment! What we have tasted of Christ and his daily blessings already is only a taster of the glorious banquet and happy life that await us. Our 'daily bread' is a reminder that we shall soon be feasting with Jesus in his kingdom.

Jesus often spoke of this wonderful occasion, when our Father will host his people at the wedding supper for his Son's marriage to his bride, the church. This is not just a material feast, but a spiritual feast in which we will fully enjoy the blessings of our Father's provision of his Son, the bread of life. In the Lord's Prayer we ask the Father to 'save us a place' at this banquet!

'Give us today our daily bread' is therefore a request for God's sustaining nourishment of our material, spiritual and eternal needs through Jesus Christ.

We ask our Father to give us our daily bread *today*

As we pray this prayer, we are conscious of depending upon God every day. Like small children, we need our Father constantly. This is the kind of close relationship our heavenly Father wants. A caring father wouldn't show his children a huge larder full of food and tell them, 'There you are, kids, help yourselves to whatever you need. I'll see you in a year or two and check how you're getting on!' Instead, he would be with them every day, always aware of their needs, and always ready to provide for them. So it is with God. We should come to him every day to ask for 'daily bread', knowing that he will supply whatever we really need.

God is not like a mail-order company with a seven-day delivery time. We can speak to him at any time of night or day to ask for the help we need, confident that he will always hear us: 'Come quickly to help me, O LORD my Saviour' (Psalm 38:22). Though daily disciplines can be really valuable, not least because they help us to pray when we don't feel like it, we don't have to restrict our prayer. After all, we're speaking to our heavenly 'Dad'! There's nothing to stop us pouring out our hearts in tears or in joy, at moments of shame or excitement, as we pray 'in the Spirit on all occasions with all kinds of prayers and requests' (Ephesians 6:18). Our Father is not the proverbial 'absent father'. He is with us 'today' to provide whatever we need.

We ask our Father to *give* us bread

At first glance, asking God to 'give us' what we ask for almost sounds a little rude. After all, we rarely speak so bluntly even to colleagues at work! But maybe this is exactly the point. We are not to think of ourselves as diplomats or lawyers negotiating a complex deal with God, but rather as beggars in simple and desperate need or as little children who can't use complicated terminology.

We are utterly dependent on our Father's generosity. But this doesn't deny that our work is part of the means of his provision. God created mankind to steward and to develop his creation: 'The LORD God took the man and put him in the Garden of Eden to work it and take care of it' (Genesis 2:15). We are intended by God both to 'work' (develop and harness the resources of the earth) and to 'care for' (protect and preserve) the precious resources entrusted to us. In many cases, mankind has failed to do the first, for example in poverty-stricken underdeveloped regions. In other cases, mankind has failed to do the second, for example in destroying rainforests. We now face the consequences in global warming.

Paul tells the Thessalonians to work: 'Make it your ambition to lead a quiet life, to mind your own business and to work with your hands, just as we told you, so that your daily life may win the respect of outsiders and so that you will not be dependent on anybody' (1 Thessalonians 4:11; 2 Thessalonians 3:11). Christians will therefore want to avoid being a burden on others, whether this means state benefits, parental support, the generosity of friends, or our churches. As far as possible, we will want to be like God – givers rather than takers.

Living 'by faith' as Christians doesn't mean relying on others to support us. It means trusting that our Father will supply our needs as we do our best to provide for ourselves and others. Work is the means by which our Father provides for our needs, 'bringing forth food from the earth: wine that gladdens the heart of man; oil to make his face shine, and bread that sustains his heart' (Psalm 104:14–15), and Christians will not be afraid of hard work, for 'he who works his land will have abundant food, but the one who chases fantasies will have his fill of poverty' (Proverbs 28:19).

Above all, asking for our bread makes us deeply grateful for whatever God gives. Recognizing that our abilities, opportunities, employment, homes and technology all come from our Father through our work, we are committed to being contented and grateful. Paul insists, 'Be joyful always; pray continually; give thanks in all circumstances, for this is God's will for you in Christ Jesus' (1 Thessalonians 5:16–18). We can thank him when we pray for our 'daily bread'.

We want bread because we are not 'ascetics'

We are not to be ascetics, denying the enjoyment of God's good creation. Such a refusal to enjoy our Father's generosity is actually 'taught by demons' (1 Timothy 4:1), even if practised by some monks and nuns. Such religious principles, however impressive, 'lack any value in restraining sensual indulgence' (Colossians 2:23). The tragic failure of many who have taken unnatural vows of chastity is evidence of this folly. Paul tells Timothy that we are required to sanctify our enjoyment of creation by enjoying things in accordance with biblical principles and with thankful prayer.

We will be ready to sacrifice material comforts, not because God wants us to enjoy pain, but when it is necessary for the good of others. This is what Jesus meant when he said, 'If anyone would come after me, he must deny himself and take up his cross and follow me' (Mark 8:34). He didn't mean that we should live a life as devoid of comfort and pleasure as possible, but that we should be ready to sacrifice everything for the salvation of others. Christ did not go to the cross because he liked pain. He was no masochist. He suffered on the cross because it was necessary for his mission and the gospel. So we are free to enjoy all good things in grateful purity, but must be ready to make sacrifices for the good of others, especially their salvation.

We ask our Father to give *us* bread

When we pray, Jesus wants us to remember our Christian brothers and sisters who need his provision. We are not to pray 'Give me my bread', but 'Give *us* our bread'. And when he answers our prayer, what he gives is for 'us' to share with others. And so we work not only for ourselves, but so as to 'have something to share with those in need' (Ephesians 4:28).

The desperate need of the world's poor may seem beyond our ability to deal with, but we can all try to help those for whom we are responsible, namely our families, our churches, gospel ministry and the poor we come across:

We pray for 'bread' to share with our families

We don't want to neglect our families, for, 'if anyone does not provide for his relatives, and especially for his immediate family, he has denied the faith and is worse than an unbeliever' (1 Timothy 5:8).

And we must be careful not to leave our family neglected because we have ring-fenced money for worthy causes. We could also pray about our own financial needs in this section of the Lord's Prayer.

We pray for 'bread' to share with our church

We want to share our resources with our local church. The early church was quick to see this opportunity for mutual love: 'No-one claimed that any of his possessions was his own, but they shared everything they had . . . There were no needy persons among them . . . ' (Acts 4:32–34). Though they clearly didn't sell all their houses and possessions (this was no communist or charity-dependent commune), they were very generous in ensuring that no-one was neglected. We could pray about the financial needs of our church in the Lord's Prayer.

We pray for 'bread' to share with gospel ministries

We want to share our resources with those in gospel ministry. Paul could claim, 'You . . . know that these hands of mine have supplied my own needs and the needs of my companions. In everything I did, I showed you that by this kind of hard work we must help the weak, remembering the words the Lord Jesus himself said: "It is more blessed to give than to receive"' (Acts 20:34–35). Christians will take pleasure in being able to support gospel workers. It is a joyful privilege to share what God provides with ministry apprentice-trainees, pastor-teachers and evangelist-missionaries who need our help, and we can pray for these resources in the Lord's Prayer.

We pray for 'bread' to share with the poor

We want to share our resources with Christians elsewhere. Paul cites the Macedonian churches as an example to the Corinthians, because, 'out of the most severe trial, their overflowing joy and their extreme poverty welled up in rich generosity . . . they urgently pleaded with us for the privilege of sharing in this service' (2 Corinthians 8:2–4). We cannot claim to be real Christians and remain uncaring towards needy Christians. 'Suppose a brother or sister is without clothes and daily food. If one of you says to him, "Go, I wish you well; keep warm and well fed," but does nothing about his physical needs, what good is it? In the same way, faith by itself, if it is not accompanied by action, is dead' (James 2:15–17). We could pray for Christians in needy parts of the world at this point.

And we are to share our resources with those in need, the 'poor at our gate'. 'If a man shuts his ears to the cry of the poor, he too will cry out and not be answered' (Proverbs 21:13; 29:7). Indeed, if our enemy is hungry, we should feed him (Proverbs 25:21). Though the needs of the whole world are too daunting for us to address, Jesus taught in his parable of the Good Samaritan (Luke 10) that the neighbour we should love sacrificially is whomever we come across who needs our help. He himself is, of course, the 'Great' Samaritan, the finest example of such costly love.

When we ask for our daily bread, we are asking for 'our' daily bread to share with others, for 'a generous man will himself be blessed, for he shares his bread with the poor' (Proverbs 22:9). Is there any more convincing proof, for unbelievers and believers alike, of the Holy Spirit's deep transformation of an individual or a church as when Christians open their wallets, wisely but generously, for the unemployed, the sick and those ravaged by debt in the church and in the local community?

We ask only for 'bread'

Whilst we are not 'bread-rejecting ascetics', we are also not 'cake-demanding hedonists'! By teaching us to ask for 'bread' (basic necessities), rather than 'cake' (desirable luxuries), Jesus is teaching us to be content with a modest standard of living. This is a petition for our needs and not our greeds! In a Western materialistic culture, where people worship on Sunday mornings at IKEA, Tesco and car-boot sales, this is counter-cultural. Jesus talked of the 'deceitfulness of wealth' (Mark 4:19), because wealth seems to promise happiness and security but delivers neither. Of course, money can help solve lots of superficial problems, but it can't provide the joy and security deep in our souls that Christ alone can provide. Those who are in Christ can therefore break free from the relentless drive for wealth and the vain search for a 'quality of life' that can be known only in heaven.

We must recognize the dangers of 'cake', and that 'godliness with contentment is great gain. For we brought nothing into the world, and we can take nothing out of it. But if we have food and clothing, we will be content with that. People who want to get rich fall into temptation and a trap and into many foolish and harmful desires that plunge men into ruin and destruction. For the love of money is a root of all kinds of evil. Some people, eager for money, have wandered from the faith and pierced themselves with many griefs. But you, man of God, flee from all this . . . ' (1 Timothy 6:6–11).

For most of us, perhaps the wisdom of Proverbs captures the modest lifestyle with which we can be well content, and to which Jesus refers in his prayer: 'Give me neither poverty nor riches, but give me only my **daily bread**. Otherwise, I may have too much and disown you and say, "Who is the Lord?" Or I may become poor and steal, and so dishonour the name of my God' (Proverbs 30:8–9).

We ask our Father confidently

We have Jesus' marvellous reassurance that we shall be well provided for. He said, 'Which of you, if his son asks for bread, will give him a stone? . . . how much more will your Father in heaven give good gifts to those who ask him!' (Matthew 7:9, 11). Away with cynicism! Our loving Father will generously provide all we need materially, spiritually and eternally. And he will give only gifts that are good for us in becoming like Christ.

As earthly fathers love to be generous, so too we find our Father being extravagant. I always find it entertaining that God provided the grumbling Israelites not only with manna, but also with quails so they could have meat in the evenings as well as bread in the morning. How did God get so much fresh meat to a vast nomadic people in the desert? He flew it in! Every evening, a huge flock of quails arrived for the Israelites to kill and eat. How true it is that, when we ask 'Give us this day our daily bread', our Father usually seems to throw in some quails as well!

Jesus teaches us to enjoy our Father

as our DAILY PROVIDER
. . . AS NEEDY BEGGARS

So how might we pray this in practice?

Caz arrived back at her flat before the others. It was nearly 10.30pm but usually no-one was back before 11.00, so Caz enjoyed a long soak in the bath and then settled onto the sitting room sofa in front of the TV with a glass of Chardonnay. She knew she was falling in love. Guy wasn't the best-looking man she'd ever seen. But it was amazing how knowing him was making him more attractive. All the way home she'd been chewing over his ideas for going to Bible college and then heading out to Vietnam with

One World. He'd grown up in Indonesia and felt comfortable in South-East Asia. And he'd done a short-service placement in Phnom Penh, and as they'd talked that evening, she began to realize that he was very serious. In fact she eventually twigged that he was testing her willingness to go with him. Marriage – AAAAAAAAAAH! She closed her eyes once more into the Lord's Prayer . . .

'Our Father . . . give us this day our daily bread . . . '

'Father, thank you for always providing for my needs. Thank you for my family and job and flat and church and friends and especially for Guy who makes me so happy right now . . . er . . .

'Please forgive me for always moaning about men in the past. Father, if this is the man you were keeping me for, sorry for being so impatient and rude to you about feeling lonely these last few years.

'Thank you that, if it is your will for me to marry Guy and go to Vietnam with him, you will provide for all my physical and spiritual and eternal needs. Please help me to trust you for everything, even when it seems scary, and to remember that I depend on your Word to provide what I need, day by day.

'Father – please give me Guy as a husband, if that's good for me becoming like Christ – I certainly feel like he would help me to be godly; and, if that means going to Vietnam, please provide all the emotional strength I'll need to support him as a wife. Please give me the spiritual strength I'll need even as a young Christian to contribute to gospel work in Vietnam. I wouldn't have a clue what to do, Father – please look after me.

'And please provide my eternal needs for life with Jesus. Please keep me spiritually alive in him and his sacrifice now and in heaven. Please feed and nourish me with Jesus, as your bread from heaven, so that I can be a

good wife and mother and missionary or whatever . . .
And if it's your will that Guy and I don't get married,
please give me strength to cope with that and serve you
as a single woman anywhere you want me. Father, please
provide physical and spiritual and eternal strength for
Guy as well, and also, Father, for your people everywhere
. . . especially in Vietnam, Father, in Jesus' name. Amen.'

Caz sat back and pondered what an incredible day it
had been. The Lord's Prayer was amazing, and she wasn't
finished with it yet! Someone else had arrived . . .

And meanwhile . . .
Sylvie stared with red-eyed exhaustion at her Sunday
school teachers' notes on the Lord's Prayer. Her class of
seven-to-eight-year-olds were thoroughly enjoying it so
far, but she'd have to be creative to keep their attention.
After a long day with the local comprehensive school's
sixth form and an evening cooking, she was cream-
crackered. It was already 10.30, but with so little time to
prepare before Sunday, she had to try to concentrate. She
loved the Lord's Prayer. Her father had prayed it every
day and taught it to her as a child.

Pastor Jack's *Lessons from Jesus' Prayer* were good so far:
'Adoption into God's family', 'Respect is due', 'Return of
the King' and 'God's Extreme Makeover' had worked
well. How would 'Bread of Heaven' go down, especially
with the Franklin twins? They were a handful. If she
could find some good ideas she could use them in a
school assembly soon as well. The other teachers were
always glad when she volunteered. She thought the
Lord's Prayer would work well for the school, being part
of our English heritage and culture and having been
prayed at Diana's funeral – surely no-one could possibly
object. As a fifty-eight-year-old mother of four who'd

been teaching for thirty years, Sylvie found the new
politically correct atmosphere hard to understand.

She thought about holding up a loaf of bread for the
Sunday school class and asking what it symbolized. She
could tell the story of the manna and perhaps find a
Welsh male-voice choir singing that rugby song, 'Bread
of Heaven', on CD. Perhaps she could scatter Frosties®
cereal all over the floor and tell the children to pick up
enough for a bowlful. No, that would be a disastrous
mess. There was lots she could do – but she needed to
write down a prayer for the kids to use and take home.
She knew that some Christian parents were using these
prayers at Sunday lunch, and she always prayed that the
unbelieving parents might understand the gospel through
her weekly worksheets. She reckoned that the Sunday
school teachers were doing more evangelism in their
classes than any of the other church teachers. And she
did love telling the kids from the estate about Jesus,
especially the Franklins.

She tried to write a simple prayer:

'Our Father in heaven . . . Give us today our daily bread . . . '

'Thank you for giving us bread for physical life – for
meals, sweets and shops. Thank you for giving us bread
for spiritual life – for Jesus dying on the cross. Thank you
for giving us bread for eternal life – to bring us to your
'party' in heaven. And please help us to be willing to
share all these resources with poor people everywhere.
Amen.'

She knew that some of the kids would struggle with
the idea of different kinds of bread. But she could cut out
big cardboard bread slices with pictures of toast, a cross
and a party to reinforce the prayer – that should work
well. She would soon have a really good series for school.
This prayer seemed such a culturally acceptable way to

teach the Christian faith, revealing God as loving Father, ruling Lord and gracious Saviour. Sylvie spent the next hour cutting and painting cardboard, but also rejoicing that the Lord's Prayer was for kids as well as scholars, before she staggered off to join her sleeping husband in bed, weary but sensing the approval of her heavenly Father.

7 'Forgive us our debts . . .'

(Needing our Father's pardon)

The second triplet of petitions in the Lord's Prayer are all linked by the little word 'and'. Unlike the first three petitions, which can be considered separately, the second three are interdependent because we couldn't survive without any of them. Praise God that he not only gives bread, but also forgives sins and delivers from evil. Imagine a British soldier captured by the Taliban in Afghanistan. For this soldier to be of any further use in Her Majesty's army, he would need the provision of three things: nourishment to stay alive, liberation from captivity and protection from enemy forces – in other words, resources, deliverance and safety. Likewise, Christians need resources of daily bread (provision), deliverance from sin (pardon) and safety from Satan (protection) all at the same time if we are to be of any use in the service of our Lord Jesus Christ.

The fifth petition of the Lord's Prayer, 'Forgive us our debts', is a request for our Father's pardon and deliverance from sin. This petition is simultaneously an expression of faith, a confession of sins and a commitment to forgive.

'Forgive us our debts' is an expression of faith in Christ

When we pray 'Forgive us our debts', we are expressing our faith in the work of Christ on the cross. The Bible teaches three major and complementary perspectives on how our forgiveness was achieved, each with an important Old Testament background. In a pivotal sentence in Paul's magnificent letter to the Romans, we find all three:

> All have sinned and fall short of the glory of God, and are **justified** freely by his grace through the **redemption** that came by Christ Jesus. God presented him as a **propitiation** through faith in his blood.
> (Romans 3:23–25, ESV)

In Christ we are 'justified' – the language of the law court
To 'justify' someone is to declare them 'righteous'. God cannot allow unrighteous people into his presence in heaven. In order to justify unrighteous people like us, God must reckon to us the righteous obedience of his Son, Jesus. The righteousness of Christ's perfect Christian life is counted as ours because he lived it as our representative, the true Adam. The righteousness of God that Paul has in mind is not only the righteousness of God's character in saving us, but also the gift of God in Christ by which we are acceptable to God (Romans 5:19 and 10:4).

This was foretold in a famous 'Suffering Servant' song promising Jesus, where we read 'by his knowledge [lit., knowledge of him] my righteous servant will justify many' (Isaiah 53:11). The servant who is righteous (Jesus) will provide the righteousness for many who know him by faith (us).

Christ 'shrank himself' down to become an ordinary man in order to *swap* places with ordinary people like us on the cross, because he loves us so passionately. On the cross, Christ was treated as if he were us (punished for our sins) so that we can be treated as if we were him (accepted or 'justified' as perfect sons). Paul explains, 'God made him who had no sin [Jesus] to be sin for us [on the cross], so that in him [by faith] we might become the righteousness of God [justified]' (2 Corinthians 5:21). This is not merely being declared 'not guilty', but being declared positively righteous and fit for heaven.

We already know that our life in Christ is acceptable, because our life in him has already been raised from the dead: 'He was delivered over to death for our sins and was raised to life for our justification' (Romans 4:25). The life that qualifies us for heaven is already seated at the right hand of the Father in Christ. We are saved because our sins have been punished in Christ and the righteousness we need has been lived in Jesus, in his obedience unto death. To be justified is to be counted by God 'just-as-if-I'd-been-Jesus'.

Charles Dickens' classic novel *A Tale of Two Cities* provides us with an apt illustration of this sensational 'swap'. The story is set in the late eighteenth century during the French Revolution. Two men, Charles Darnay (a French aristocrat) and Sydney Carton (a rotten English lawyer), who happen to look very similar, fall in love with the same woman. She loves only Darnay, but Darnay is captured and imprisoned in Paris, and sentenced to be executed by guillotine. So, out of love for the girl, Carton does the one good thing he has ever done. He goes to the prison with a friend. They drug Darnay, and Carton exchanges clothes with him, and Darnay is taken out to a carriage in Carton's clothes and with Carton's papers travels through the barricades around Paris and safely home to his wife and child in England. The next day, Sydney Carton is executed in Charles Darnay's place.

Christ was executed in our place so that we can come back to the Father, clothed in his righteousness, entitled to his privileges as sons of God. He swapped places with us to be treated like us so we can be treated like him. Isaiah described the joy of being reckoned justified in the sight of God: 'I delight greatly in the LORD; my soul rejoices in my God. For he has clothed me with garments of salvation and arrayed me in a robe of righteousness' (Isaiah 61:10).

It was this discovery by the European Reformers that God's righteousness is not only what our Father is, but what our Father gives in Christ, that exposed the errors of the medieval Roman Catholic Church. It remains vital today to realize that God's grace is not the power of the Spirit received through the sacraments to become righteous enough to be justified (as Rome still teaches). God's grace is his gift of all that we need for salvation in Christ. Clothed in his righteousness, we are perfectly acceptable to our Father (and the Holy Spirit gradually changes us to become like Christ because we are already saved in him). When we pray 'Forgive us our sins', we ask God to remember that we are 'justified' by his grace through faith in Christ.

In Christ we have 'redemption' – the language of the slave market
Though the redemption of slaves was familiar in the Roman culture of Jesus' day, the background to this liberation from slavery upon the payment of a ransom was the exodus from Egypt. The death of a sacrificial lamb was the ransom price for the life of each oldest son in Israel. Where the blood of the sacrifice was placed over the homes of these boys, God's wrath at the idolatry of Egypt (in which Israel shared) was satisfied and his judgment 'passed over' that house.

God had promised, 'I am the LORD. The blood will be a sign for you on the houses where you are; and when I see the blood, I will pass over you. No destructive plague will touch you when I strike Egypt. This is a day you are to commemorate' (Exodus 12:12–14).

In fulfilment of this redemption of Israel, Christ died as our sacrificial lamb, so that we who are in Christ, the firstborn sons and heirs of the kingdom, could be redeemed: 'For Christ, our Passover lamb, has been sacrificed' (1 Corinthians 5:7). For this reason it is significant that Christ, the 'lamb of God', was dying on the cross just as the sacrificial lambs were being slaughtered for the Feast of Passover in the Temple of Jerusalem. We are set free both from Satan's power and from the wrath we deserve from God by Christ's blood painted over our lives, for, 'we have redemption through his blood' (Ephesians 1:7).

In 1995, when Philip Lawrence, headmaster of St George's School in Maida Vale, London, walked out into the street to find a pupil being set upon by a gang of thugs, he acted to rescue the poor boy. But when he intervened to save the lad from the gang, he was punched and fatally stabbed. After staggering back into his school, he bled to death. Perhaps that pupil did not previously care much for his headmaster – few schoolboys will put a poster of their headmaster on their bedroom wall. But from that day on, the boy's attitude to Philip Lawrence would forever be different, as he had 'redeemed' his life from a violent gang at the cost of his own life. Indeed, the Philip Lawrence Awards scheme has been established to help encourage positive initiatives among young people. In the same way, Christ came into our world to 'redeem' us from the gang of thugs called Satan, Sin and Death, at the cost of his appalling death on the cross. When we realize that he did this not just for other people but for you and me, we will want to be involved in the positive initiatives that honour him!

When we pray 'Forgive us our sins', we ask God to remember that he has ransomed us from slavery to Satan, sin and eternal death.

In Christ we have a 'propitiation' – the language of the temple

The satisfaction or 'propitiation' of God's personal justice was established as a condition of being cleansed ('sanctified') for God's presence under the sacrificial laws of Leviticus for Israel. The climax of the atonement ceremonies for this cleansing was the Day of Atonement (Leviticus 16). The High Priest entered into the presence of God in the tabernacle to sacrifice two goats, to symbolize twin aspects of this 'propitiation' of God. One goat was killed to satisfy God that a death had taken place for the guilty. Sin had been punished. Another goat had the sins of the people confessed over its head and was driven out to die in the desert as a 'scapegoat', carrying the guilt of the people. Sin had been taken away.

In fulfilment of this ceremony, Christ entered the heavenly presence of God as our eternal High Priest with the blood, not of animals, but of his own self-sacrifice: 'When this priest had offered for all time one sacrifice for sins, he sat down at the right hand of God . . . by one sacrifice he has made perfect for ever those who are being made holy' (Hebrews 10:12–13). God has been satisfied so his wrath is diverted away and the record of our sin has been taken away as far as the East is from the West, once and for all time on the cross. In God's eyes, we are now cleansed from any stain of corruption or guilt. As God had promised, 'Though your sins are like scarlet, they shall be as white as snow' (Isaiah 1:18). When we pray 'Forgive us our sins', we ask God to remember that he has been propitiated by the death of Christ, so we are morally clean.

Through the death of Christ in our place on the cross, we are **acceptable** by justification, **free** by redemption and **clean** by propitiation. On this basis, our debts to God are completely forgiven and pardoned.

His death was a 'penal substitution'

Common to all three of these perspectives on the death of Christ is his amazing willingness to suffer the penalty due for our sins in our place as a kind of 'lightning conductor', drawing God's wrath away from us and onto himself on the cross. This is called 'penal subsititutionary atonement'. Perhaps the clearest, and because of Handel's *Messiah* the most familiar, articulation of this truth comes in the central stanza of Isaiah 53: 'But he was pierced for our transgressions, he was crushed for our iniquities; the punishment that brought us peace was upon him, and by his wounds we are healed. We all, like sheep, have gone astray, each of us has turned to his own way; and the LORD has laid on him the iniquity of us all.'

One may illustrate this self-sacrifice with human acts of heroism such as that of Major Mike Wills, a Royal Marine parachuting instructor, in June 2004. A *Daily Telegraph* report reads, 'A teenager survived a plane crash when an Army major shielded him with his body as the aircraft nose-dived, an inquest heard yesterday. Daniel Greening was strapped to Royal Marine instructor Mike Wills when the light plane's engine failed as they took part in a charity sky-dive in Devon. As it plummeted, Major Wills sacrificed himself by putting his back to the metalwork and taking the brunt of the impact – shielding the 16-year-old boy with his body' (Telegraph. co.uk, 31.7.07). This was clearly an act of heroic self-sacrifice. It's striking that the teenager who survived joined the Air Training Corps and trained as a pilot after making a full recovery.

In a similar way, Christ took upon himself the 'brunt of the impact' of the penalty for our sin when he died on the cross for his people. (And, as Daniel Greening took up flying, so we are expected to take up the way of our Saviour, in lives of sacrificial service.) Christ's sacrifice involved suffering not only the physical crash of the cross, but the spiritual suffering of hell, and he did this for us when we were not his friends but his enemies, and he even did it although he is so great and we are so offensive. Best of all, he is the only one who has done it for us!

There have always been critics of this glorious truth among those who don't like the Bible's teaching about God's wrath and punishment of sinners. A Dean of St Alban's Cathedral in England once called this teaching 'repulsive' and 'insane'.[1] Others have described it as 'cosmic child abuse'.[2] The accusation is that for Jesus to be punished for our sin is unjust, both because an innocent man was punished for what he didn't do and because God should not have forced a third party to suffer for the guilty. This accusation fails on both counts to recognize that Jesus is the genuine representative of sinful people. We were 'in him' when he died on the cross, for 'one died for all [Christ was our substitute], and therefore all died [Christ was also our representative]' (2 Corinthians 5:14).

Let me illustrate. If I were playing football, badly, for England at Wembley Stadium, the coach would be wise to send a substitute onto the pitch to take my place. If Steven Gerrard, the iconic Liverpool captain, came on in my place, he would be my 'substitute'. He plays instead of me. And if he scores a goal, I can jump up, shouting, 'We've scored'. Only one man kicked the ball into the goal, but we all benefit because he represented us. He is both our substitute and our representative. In the same way, although Christ suffered instead of me as my substitute, I was also punished for my sins in him because he is my representative. I can jump up shouting, 'I've already been punished for my sins and my judgment is completed . . . in Jesus.'

Moreover, he was not a third party unjustly forced by God into this representative role, for God himself was 'reconciling the world to himself in Christ' (2 Corinthians 5:19). God took his own wrath upon himself in order to be just. Furthermore, the Son was never 'picked on' by the Father as an unwilling victim. He was a loving, adult volunteer. He came to be our representative to freely offer himself up to capture, torture, execution and hell. God the Son gave himself to suffer our penalty because he loves us so much.

'Forgive us our debts' is a confession of sins to God

When we pray 'Forgive us our sins', we admit to God that we need his forgiveness. On this occasion, when Jesus taught the Lord's Prayer, he called sin 'our debts', emphasizing our failure to give God what is due to him. (The word 'trespasses', used in more traditional versions of the Lord's Prayer, is another biblical idea meaning law-breaking.) On the occasion recorded in Luke, he called sin 'our sins', a word emphasizing our failure to reach the standard expected of us by God. Both words stress our failure to honour and obey God as he deserves. When we pray the Lord's Prayer, we have to admit that we are spiritual failures.

Imagine that two young teachers, Ricky and Brian, were looking to share a flat in south London. They scoured the internet, fearing exorbitant prices, and suddenly came across this amazing advert: 'Palatial mansion in twenty acres of mature gardens overlooking Wimbledon Common: ten stately reception rooms, fourteen bedrooms on two floors, swimming pool, games room, wet room, snooker room – two tenants needed – £10 per month for two years.' Assuming such an incredible offer could only be a misprint, the excited pair called the number, only to discover that the offer was genuine! The owner was a Russian billionaire going home for a couple of years on business, wanting responsible tenants to care for his estate. He didn't need money. The only thing he asked was that they keep in touch to discuss the needs of the property. The owner departed and the two young men moved in, ecstatic at their good fortune.

Ricky and Brian proved to be very different. Ricky moved into the top floor, and very soon fifty wild friends had moved in with him. All-night parties, beer stains on the walls, cigarette burns on the furniture, vomit on the carpets – the whole floor was soon trashed. It was obvious that, when the owner returned, Ricky would be thrown out in disgrace.

Brian was totally different. He took the middle floor and was impeccably behaved. In bed by ten each night, he washed the windows every Tuesday, polished the door handles every Thursday, and licked the floor spotless every weekend. He was so neat and tidy he even had turn-ups in his pyjamas! Everyone assumed that, when the owner returned, Brian would be declared the perfect tenant and invited to stay for ever.

When the billionaire returned, to everyone's surprise he kicked them both out. To any who cared to ask, he sadly explained, 'To be sure, Ricky trashed the place while Brian was incredibly tidy, but both men utterly failed me in different ways. Neither bothered to stay in touch, though I left them countless messages. They ignored my requests and treated me with contempt. I'm afraid they abused my kindness by failing to remember whose house they were living in. They seemed to forget I even existed. Oh, and they failed to pay any rent!'

This illustrates how different people fail God. We all live in God's beautiful creation. He supplies us richly with so much to enjoy. He expects us to stay in touch, listen to his messages and remember that we live in his world. But in different ways we ignore him and abuse his generosity. Some people trash their lives. The wreckage of spoiled relationships is everywhere. Such people generally know that they are in trouble with God. Others are so neat and tidy, so refined and polite, so religious and moral, that we're very surprised to hear that God should throw *them* out of his presence for ever and into hell. But we've all failed to treat God with the respect and gratitude that his generosity deserves. After a lifetime of telling God to 'push off and leave us alone', in hell we'll discover the true horror of what we've so arrogantly demanded.

We owe a massive debt to God because we've failed to live up to the standards he is entitled to expect from us. Paul writes, 'Do you show contempt for the riches of his kindness, tolerance and patience, not realising that God's kindness leads you to repentance? But because of your stubbornness and your unrepentant heart, you are storing up wrath against yourself for the day of God's wrath, when his righteous judgment will be revealed . . . for those who are self-seeking and who reject the truth and follow evil, there will be wrath and anger' (Romans 2:4–8). Our debt to him just gets bigger every day and there is nothing we can do to make up for it.

Praying 'Forgive us our debts' brings us the joy of recalling God's gracious pardon, while unconfessed sin leaves us burdened with guilt and feeling distant from our Father. King David knew this well: 'When I kept silent, my bones wasted away through my groaning all day long. For day and night your hand was heavy upon me; my strength was sapped as in the heat of summer. Then I acknowledged my sin to you and did not cover up my iniquity. I said, "I will confess my transgressions to the LORD" – and you forgave the guilt of my sin' (Psalm 32:3–5). We don't say this to remind God of our dependence on him but to remind ourselves. Indeed, we are forgiven through faith in Christ, not through the regularity of our confession. In any case, we will never be able to confess all our sins, for many are forgotten or unknown. But confession of any sins reminds us of God's marvellous grace and draws us closer to him. If we confess our sins, we can experience the relief and delight of a renewed relationship with our Father: 'If we claim to be without sin, we deceive ourselves and the truth is not in us. If we confess our sins, he is faithful and just and will forgive us our sins and purify us from all unrighteousness' (1 John 1:8–9).

I don't think Christians need to be overly obsessed with confession, for we are after all completely forgiven from the moment we place our faith in Christ for our salvation! But confessing our sins does humble our pride and reassure us of God's marvellous grace. So it is surprising how few churches still confess their sins to the Father in their Sunday meetings. If they prayed the Lord's Prayer, this deficiency would be rectified. When we ask our Father 'Forgive us our debts', whether privately or corporately, we are confessing our need of his pardon, and seeking the joy of his reassurance that our sins are forgiven.

'Forgive us our debts' is a commitment to forgive others

The request 'Forgive us our debts' is followed by the words 'as we also have forgiven our debtors'. At the end of the prayer, Jesus amplifies, 'For if you forgive men when they sin against you, your heavenly Father will also forgive you. But if you do not forgive men their sins, your Father will not forgive your sins'

(Matthew 6:14–15). It is the only petition he amplifies, which emphasizes its importance.

Jesus is not saying that our forgiveness of others earns our own forgiveness. That would contradict all that he and the Bible say about forgiveness being a gift of God's grace. But Jesus is plainly saying that if we are not forgiving the sins of others, we are not forgiven. Forgiveness of others is a condition of forgiveness from Christ.

There are two aspects to this willingness to forgive. The first is that a willingness to forgive is the inevitable impact of being forgiven through Christ. We could not truly believe the gospel that Christ died for our sins if that did not alter our treatment of those who sin against us.

The second aspect of this condition is that forgiving others is part of the repentance required of anyone becoming a Christian. Forgiveness is always conditional upon repentance, of which forgiving others is a part. Jesus simply will not forgive those who are unwilling to forgive others.

Our capacity to forgive others is granted to us by God, and, like other areas of our repentance, will never be perfect or consistent. Forgiveness of others, especially when their wrongdoing has been very serious, is usually a process that takes time and will include better and worse periods. Those who have been abused by a parent or betrayed by a partner will know this struggle well. But, as with repentance from immorality or greed, we must try. We cannot ourselves be reassured that we are forgiven if we are not trying to forgive others.

Jesus told an important parable to illustrate his meaning (Matthew 18:21–35). He described a king who cancelled an enormous debt owed by a servant, who then went out and began to strangle a fellow servant who owed him a very small amount. When the king heard of it, he seized the unmerciful servant and said, '"You wicked servant . . . I cancelled all that debt of yours because you begged me to. Shouldn't you have had mercy on your fellow-servant just as I had on you?" In anger his master turned him over to the jailers to be tortured, until he should pay back all he owed.' Jesus concluded with chilling words, 'This is how my heavenly Father will treat each of you unless you forgive your brother from your heart.' The basis upon which we are to forgive others is that we have been forgiven so much more by our Father than we shall ever have to forgive in others. That is why Jesus replied to Peter's question about forgiving a brother up to seven times, 'I tell you, not seven times, but seventy-seven times' (18:22). We find it hard to forgive someone who is repeatedly hurting us. But our Father has forgiven us much more.

I heard this graphically illustrated when interviewing a man called James, a Christian worker in Nigeria for many years. One night he and his wife were attacked in their compound by a gang of thieves and James was shot in the face. He was airlifted home to the UK and very nearly died. After years of operations that have left him with a glass eye, a disfigured face and a permanent limp, he returns repeatedly to Nigeria to continue serving Christ. When I asked how he coped with such suffering and injustice, he said that God had enabled him to entrust his attackers to his judgment and to remember that he had himself been forgiven far more by God than he was required to forgive even in his attackers. It is the awareness of the horror of our own crimes against God that enables us to pardon the offences of others.

We must be ready to forgive the unrepentant

However, this does raise the question of whether we must forgive the unrepentant. In the *Daily Telegraph* of 3 May 2007, an article appeared under the heading 'Tebbit refuses to meet the Brighton bomber' and subtitled 'Why he cannot forgive Magee'. The article reported Lord Tebbit's unwillingness to take part in a Radio 4 programme called *The Reunion*, in which the IRA terrorist Patrick

Magee would meet some of the victims of his bomb attack on the Conservative Party Conference in Brighton in 1984.

Magee had intended to kill the Prime Minister, Mrs Thatcher, and as many of her colleagues as possible. He failed in his main purpose, but did kill five and wounded many, including Lord Tebbit, and his wife, who was permanently paralysed and confined to a wheelchair. Magee was released from prison in 1999 under the Good Friday Agreement after serving only thirteen years of his life sentence. Lord Tebbit refused the invitation in some distress, protesting that he could not possibly forgive the unrepentant Magee for his terrible crimes. 'I am weary of explaining that forgiveness is not a one-way street. The transgressor cannot be forgiven unless he acknowledges the evil of what he has done, showing remorse and repentance,' he said. 'Of course, I expect to be reminded of Christ's injunction to forgive our enemies. But I have to remember that on the Cross He asked God to forgive them because "they know not what they do". Magee knew. Because he did not repent, others have died. I can no more forgive a sinner who does not repent than a priest. That is a matter for God. The sooner Mr Magee meets Him the better.'

One can surely understand Lord Tebbit's strength of feeling. Friends were killed, he was injured, and his wife is imprisoned in her wheelchair. But was he right that forgiveness is conditional upon repentance?

I recall, by contrast, the reaction of the family of PC Stephen Oake, a Christian policeman killed in January 2003. Stephen was stabbed to death while arresting an Al Qaeda terrorist in the Crumpsall district of Manchester, leaving a wife and three children to grieve, supported by their church in Poynton. Stephen's father was reported as saying, 'I am praying for the fellow who stabbed Steve. I am praying hard to forgive, as I know Steve would have done.' When one of the Oake family appeared on the *Kilroy* television show to explain how Christ was helping them to forgive Stephen's murderer, other victims of crime invited onto the show protested that, while the Christian faith of the Oake family might be enabling them to forgive, they could not do so. There was a vivid contrast between those with the Spirit of Jesus in them and those without.

This has enormous personal implications for many people who have suffered abuse and hurt. Many are tortured by a bitter sense of grievance. What is the way forward?

There are strong arguments for forgiving only the repentant. Jesus said, 'If your brother sins, rebuke him and if he repents, forgive him. If he sins against you seven times in a day, and seven times comes back to you and says, "I repent", forgive him' (Luke 17:3–4). This passage talks explicitly of the need for repentance.

When Paul writes, 'Be kind and compassionate to one another, forgiving each other, just as in Christ God forgave you' (Ephesians 4:32), we are bound to remember that God's forgiveness is conditional upon our own repentance. In Jesus' parable, the king forgave his servant only when he came begging for forgiveness. The Prodigal Son was on his way home when he was met by the Father (Luke 15). Since God gives repentance to us, we should do all in our power to enable others to repent. Some would then argue that Jesus asked the Father to 'forgive them for they know not what they do', that is, without repentance. But Jesus was not implying that they could be saved without the Father's helping them to repent.

Putting the texts together, it seems that a relationship can be properly restored only when the wrongdoer shows some repentance and desire for reconciliation. A relationship is not restored if only one party is reconciled. However, as God has done everything to enable us to repent, we must do everything in our power to facilitate the repentance of those who hurt us, and be willing to accept even meagre expressions of repentance and sorrow, for this is how God has treated us. This may require us to explain to someone else how they have hurt us so they can apologize, though they may never recognize the full extent of their guilt. It may involve accepting very weak indications of a desire for reconciliation, with little regret expressed.

And where someone shows no willingness to change yet, we must be ready to forgive, as God is ready. We must entrust all judgment to our Father, and, like the Father in the parable of the Prodigal Son, wait patiently for signs of reconciliation and welcome the repentant without recrimination. This does not mean that all damaged relationships should be restored to a previous condition. A wife repeatedly cheated on or beaten by a drunken husband may find God's strength to forgive, without it being wise to have the man back in the home. But we must learn from Jesus, who said, 'Love your enemies and pray for those who persecute you,' even if they show no remorse. We must not seek vengeance, for God said, 'Vengeance is mine, I will repay', and he will. And we must 'bear with each other and forgive whatever grievances [we] may have against one another. Forgive as the Lord forgave [us]' (Colossians 3:13).

'Forgive us our debts' is a prayer that brings joy

The Bible has wonderful descriptions of the privilege of forgiven sin:

> I have swept away your offences like a cloud, your sins like the morning mist . . . as far as the east is from the west, so far has he removed our transgressions from us . . . You will tread our sins underfoot and hurl all our iniquities into the depths of the sea . . . Repent, then, and turn to God, so that your sins may be wiped out.
> (Isaiah 44; Psalm 103; Micah 7; Acts 3)

When we pray 'Forgive us our debts', we too can feel the intense relief and joy of remembering that all our guilt is gone, evaporated like mist, gone into space, ground into dust, lost at the bottom of the sea and deleted for ever.

The 'forgiveness of debts' generates great devotion to Jesus

Anyone who has had a huge debt paid off by a parent or friend knows how wonderful it is to be released from such a burden. When the penalty hanging over us is an eternity in hell, the relief is overwhelming: 'Blessed is he whose transgressions are forgiven' (Psalm 32:1). Such joy once overflowed in a woman who famously wept uncontrollably over Jesus as he reclined at dinner with a Pharisee named Simon (Luke 7).

She was plainly a notorious sinner, almost certainly a prostitute. She had clearly already heard Jesus' offer of forgiveness, and now she had tracked him down to express her gratitude and devotion. As the champagne glasses clinked and the guests chatted politely around the dinner table, the civilized atmosphere was suddenly ruined by this embarrassing woman. She crashed the lunch party, evidently so overcome with emotion that she couldn't speak. She began to weep over Jesus' feet and, with scandalous immodesty, let down her hair to wipe them clean. She then broke open a fabulously expensive alabaster jar of perfume, probably a precious heirloom, and poured it all over his feet, with tears streaming down her face. Simon was astonished that Jesus could allow such an immoral woman to behave so intimately and concluded that Jesus could not possibly be from God.

Perceiving his pompous thoughts, Jesus told a story about forgiven debts to explain this woman's emotions: '"Two men owed money to a certain money-lender",' Jesus began. "One owed him five hundred denarii, and the other fifty. Neither of them had the money to pay him back, so he cancelled the debts of both. Now which of them will love him more?" Simon replied, "I suppose the one who had the bigger debt cancelled." "You have judged correctly," Jesus said . . . "You did not give me any water for my feet, but she wet my feet with her tears and wiped them with her hair. You did not give me a kiss, but this woman, from the time I entered has not stopped kissing my feet. You did not put oil on my head, but she has poured perfume on my feet. Therefore, I tell you, her many sins have been forgiven – for she loved much. But he who has been forgiven little loves little"' (Luke 7:41–47).

It is very striking how perceptive Jesus is about this woman's feelings and how accepting of her tenderness, despite the embarrassing social circumstances. It is important to notice that he does not diminish her sin. He recognizes that she has committed 'many sins' and owes a big 'debt' to God. He describes her forgiveness as the cancellation of that debt. This meant that the huge cost must be borne by the lender. Jesus would shortly bear this dreadful cost himself in the humiliating agonies of crucifixion. He simply observes that those who are aware of being forgiven a lot will love Jesus a lot. Devotion to Jesus is proportionate to our sense of forgiveness. He is not saying that her love has earned her forgiveness, but that it was evidence of it. So anyone who is cool toward Jesus cannot have been forgiven. To have our huge debt to God cancelled generates immensely passionate devotion to Jesus. The other guests may have been more moral, but they remained unpardoned and cold. What intense relief, what overwhelming joy, what sacrificial love fills the hearts of those who know they have been forgiven much. Devotion to Jesus derives from understanding both the scale of our debt to God and the cost to Jesus of cancelling that debt.

In this fifth petition of the Lord's Prayer, Jesus teaches us to

ENJOY OUR FATHER AS THE FORGIVER
. . . OF SINNERS

So how might we pray this in practice?

Jo crashed into the flat first, clearly fed up. Caz and Jo had been friends since they'd met at secretarial college. Jo wasn't a Christian – yet – and not really very interested. She'd been in an off–on relationship with a married man for the last year and avoided discussing the matter with Caz because she knew that Caz was appalled. This bloke had been separated now from his wife and baby for a while, but Jo knew that Caz disapproved without Caz ever saying a word.

But Jo had been very low and unhappy recently, even depressed. For the first time in a while, she got herself a drink and sat down with Caz to chat. It emerged that her 'boyfriend' had finally broken up with her and had said some painful things about the way she treated men. Jo was recognizing that what he'd said was true. She even seemed to be feeling guilty. She asked Caz a direct question, the kind you can wait years to hear.

'How do you Christians cope with guilt? I know you're all very clean-living and all that, but you used to be quite a man-eater yourself before you "saw the light"! How do you get the forgiveness from God you're always on about?'

Caz was trying to hear if Jo was drunk, but actually she seemed stone-cold sober. She didn't like being called a 'man-eater', but this was a big opportunity.

'We just ask our heavenly Father to forgive us,' she said. 'For example, you know the Lord's Prayer? Well, in it we ask our Father in heaven to "Forgive us our debts as we also have forgiven our debtors."' She prayed silently for help.

'But how can God just forgive what you do wrong?'
Jo was puzzled. 'Surely that would mean you could abuse
people and then just get forgiven again.'

'Well, Jesus taught us to ask for our Father to forgive our
debts because his Son Jesus suffered the cost of it in his
death on the cross. God shrank himself down into an
ordinary man so he could swap places with ordinary people
like us. So he was treated like us and punished for our sins
on the cross, so we can be treated like him and accepted as
God's children. Our debts have been cancelled because
Christ paid them all off on the cross – so we're not guilty.'

'But what stops you just using Jesus' death to keep on
sinning?' asked Jo. She was more serious than Caz had
ever heard her before.

'Well, Jesus said we must pray "Forgive us our debts as
we forgive our debtors", because he expects those who've
been forgiven to be more forgiving of others. We're not
forgiven *because* we forgive others – rather, we forgive
others because we've been forgiven.' Caz remembered
Pastor Jack using that line a lot. 'If we're not prepared to
learn how to forgive others, like Jesus does, then Jesus is
not prepared to forgive us. Truth is, it's so great being
forgiven that we want to learn to forgive.' Caz was a bit
unsure, but this was surreal – and fantastic – talking
about forgiveness to 'hard-as-nails' Jo.

'Fair enough!' said Jo, abruptly, stubbing out her
cigarette thoughtfully. There was a long silence. Caz
didn't want to stop Jo thinking it through. She prayed
quietly, 'Father, help her to ask you to forgive her debts,
please Father.'

After a long time, Jo said quietly, 'I'd like to be forgiven
like you are. I think I'll come to church on Sunday!' And
with that she stood up and went to bed. Caz was gob-
smacked. Miracles do happen – when we pray.

And meanwhile . . .

Pastor Jack was still talking with James, who had come to see him in some distress at the end of the prayer meeting that night. Pastor Jack had begun the meeting by explaining that some months ago they'd started saying the Lord's Prayer regularly in church again, as in previous generations. He'd been giving a series of talks at the monthly prayer meetings since, each time exploring one of the petitions in the Lord's Prayer. Today's was the forgiveness of sins. He'd asked the assistant minister to delay praying the Lord's Prayer until after the talk but before the Lord's Supper, as a prayer of response and commitment. He'd been pointing out that this petition for the forgiveness of debts had both reassurance and challenge in it. While this petition reassured those who had confessed their sins that Christ's death had satisfied the Father for our justification, our redemption and our propitiation, there was also a challenge to forgive the debts of others.

He'd worked hard on the talk, knowing that some of the congregation had been hurt and abused in the past. Others had fallen out with each other recently. He didn't want to trot out trite phrases that failed to acknowledge how difficult and variable forgiveness can be. But Jesus was clear that our forgiveness is conditional upon forgiving others, and he felt worried that he'd been too lenient in the past and didn't want to imperil the congregation by being unclear. After his talk he led the congregation in the prayer he'd carefully prepared . . .

'Father . . . please forgive us our debts as we have forgiven our debtors. Father, thank you that Christ has died for the forgiveness of all our sins; for our justification to make us acceptable in his righteousness; for our redemption to deliver us from your wrath and from Satan's power; and for our propitiation that cleanses us to your satisfaction; thank you so much for forgiving our sins because Christ has paid our debt. Please help us now to forgive the debts of others, for we know that if we are to receive forgiveness we must grant forgiveness to others.

'Father, you know that many of us have suffered great wrongs. Help us to realize that we've been forgiven far more than we must forgive. Help us to forgive those who repent of their sin, and help us to be ready to forgive those who have not yet repented. Help us to love our enemies, leave vengeance to you, offer reconciliation wherever possible, and above all to genuinely pardon the debts of others. We know this is only possible by the power of your Holy Spirit, so pardon our sins and strengthen us to pardon the sins of others, whether sins of violence, neglect, prejudice, cruelty or betrayal. Please give us your strength to forgive that we too may be forgiven, in Jesus' name, in whom is both the forgiveness of sins, and the power to forgive. Amen.'

The assistant minister led the congregation in the Lord's Prayer and then the Lord's Supper. There was a great deal of discussion over coffee and not a few healing tears. And now James, the non-Christian husband, who had betrayed and left his wife, wanted to talk to Jack about being forgiven. The Lord was powerfully at work through his Prayer.

8 'Lead us . . . and deliver us . . .'

(Needing our Father's protection)

'And **lead** us not into **temptation** but **deliver** us from **the evil one.**'

Even ordinary human fathers feel hugely protective of their children. I myself recall, when my youngest son broke his arm, becoming engulfed by an intense mist of protectiveness. I was summoned to the school playground where an anxious mother met me at the gate carrying my four-year-old, who had fallen off a climbing frame. His forearm was bent at a right angle and was clearly broken. Without any word of reassurance for the poor woman, I seized my whimpering son and drove him to hospital, where I rushed into casualty and gracelessly demanded that a doctor see him *immediately*. Everyone responded magnificently, but on reflection I am shocked at how aggressively protective I had become. Any man hoping to date my daughters . . . beware!

If human fathers can feel such protective love towards their kids, could our heavenly Father possibly be remotely casual about any of his adopted children facing injury or hurt? Could our divine Father ever abandon or neglect the children for whom he gave his beloved Son on the cross? Jesus knew from personal experience that God the Father protects his children, especially from the truly frightening threat posed by Satan. And he wants his disciples to recognize our vulnerability and need of our Father's protection.

Having asked for the provision of bread and pardon for sin, the final petition asks our Almighty Father for protection from evil. In particular, we need protection from 'temptation' (trials) and from 'the evil one' (Satan).

Trials await us

The word for 'temptation' used by Jesus here is a broad word meaning 'trial'. It can refer either to spiritually positive 'testing' from God that purifies our faith or to spiritually negative 'entice-ment' by Satan that lures us into sin.

The fact that Jesus had been recently tempted to sin by Satan, together with the reference to 'the evil one', would seem to suggest that Jesus had temptation to sin in mind. But the request that the Father should not lead us into this temptation seems to contradict the statement in James that God never tempts anyone to sin: 'When tempted, no-one should say, "God is tempting me." For God cannot be tempted by evil, nor does he tempt anyone; but each one is tempted when, by his own evil desire, he is dragged away and enticed. Then, after desire has conceived, it gives birth to sin; and sin, when it is full-grown, gives birth to death' (James 1:13–15). Why would Jesus want us to ask God not to do something that he would never do anyway?

On the other hand, if this petition is asking to avoid trials that test our faith, it seems to contradict other texts that call us to welcome such testing, e.g. 'Consider it pure joy, my brothers, whenever you face trials of many kinds, because you know that the testing of your faith develops perseverance. Perseverance must finish its work so that you may be mature and complete . . . ' (James 1:2–4).

In fact, it seems best to interpret the term Jesus uses as referring to trials that either test our faith or lure us into sin, but with qualifications in each case.

Testing that purifies our faith

It is perfectly acceptable to ask to avoid painful experiences, even if we know that God can use them for good. After all, Jesus asked to avoid the cross if possible. We don't enjoy trials – they are, by definition, difficult and painful. Christians are sacrificial for the good of others, not because we are sado-masochists. We need to understand that God may send trials that are good for us, much as a good teacher will set exams to help students realize what they do and don't know, or a parent will ask a child to perform a difficult domestic chore to teach her to contribute to the good of the family even when it is costly. Likewise, we read, ' . . . for a little while you may have had to suffer grief in all kinds of trials. These have come so that your faith – of greater worth than gold, which perishes even though refined by fire – may be proved genuine and may result in praise, glory and honour when Jesus Christ is revealed' (1 Peter 1:6–7). Difficult periods of 'testing' compel us to appreciate how much we need our Father and drive us to him in faith and prayer. We know that such trials may be good for us, but we don't enjoy them.

So we should ask our Father to spare us such trials, even if we know we must try to rejoice in the value of them if he sends them. This means that we can pray for healing from cancer or disease, or for deliverance from a miserable job or boss, or for financial support or decent housing, without feeling that we should just accept pain and trouble without comment to God. But if the Lord chooses not to remove us from that testing situation, we can know that he must have purifying purposes in allowing it to continue, and try to rejoice in those purposes.

It is wonderful to know that unless our Father did have good purposes in our becoming more like Christ (who learned obedience from suffering), he would not allow our hardships to continue. Our Father is never trapped by any situation, even though we may be. He is not wringing his hands in heaven wishing he could do something to help. Either he will improve the situation out of his loving kindness, or he will allow it to persist in order to teach us to endure in obedient faith, much as a soldier can only really learn military discipline under fire rather than in the academy. Whichever our Father chooses, he ensures that 'in all things God works for the good of those who love him' (Romans 8:28). Life may be sometimes happy and sometimes excruciatingly painful, but, for the children of God, only ever good for us to become like Jesus!

I know a Christian woman who had cancer in her finger and had to have it surgically removed. She was left with unbearable 'phantom' pain that made her writhe in agony in a foetal position for long periods of every day for some years. Thankfully, this pain has largely abated now, but at the time it was unbelievably distressing for her and all the family. Yet during that period she was able to testify that her suffering brought her closer to God than ever before. She was forced to cry out to her heavenly Father for strength to endure, and found him more real and precious in her suffering than in normal life. She also had many more opportunities to speak about Jesus to concerned friends and family. Her experience reminds us that our Father sends us trials to purify our faith, even though they may involve dreadful distress and suffering. We need to realize this as we face countless lesser trials as well.

Temptation that induces us to sin

We know that Satan will try to tempt us to sin, as he has been doing from the beginnings of human history. We read of his

King's College London
New Hunt's House Library

Borrowed Items 12/03/2013 13:24
XXX8336

Item Title	Due Date

Amount Outstanding: £0.60

* Indicates items borrowed today

Item Title	Due Date
* Physical management in neurological rehabilitation	19/03/2013 23:59

Thank you for using Self-Service
www.kcl.ac.uk/library
email: libraryservices@kcl.ac.uk

familiar tactics in his sly suggestions to Eve in the garden of Eden, lies that he continues to promote in our culture today.

> Now the serpent was more crafty than any of the wild animals the LORD God had made. He said to the woman, 'Did God really say, "You must not eat . . . ?" You will not surely die . . . God knows that when you eat of it your eyes will be opened, and you will be like God, knowing good and evil.'
> (Genesis 3:1–5)

The serpent, a creature later identified as the fallen angel who is 'that ancient serpent called the devil, or Satan, who leads the whole world astray' (Revelation 12:9), induced Eve, and through her, Adam, to listen to a creature questioning the Creator. Notice his strategy.

First, he questions the reliability of the words of Scripture: 'Did God *really* say . . . ?', just as today an atheist scholar such as Richard Dawkins (author of *The God Delusion*[1]) and a popular author like Dan Brown (author of *The Da Vinci Code*[2]) openly scorn the reliability of the Bible. Satan will use their writing to tempt many people in Britain to doubt the words of God in Scripture.

Next, Satan questions the reality of judgment: 'You will not surely die . . . ', just as today people ridicule the idea that God would actually send anyone to hell to punish their evil so that we need a Saviour to suffer our agony on a cross in order to rescue us. We think we are far too nice to warrant such severity, and Satan's preachers proclaim 'Peace, peace' when there is no peace (as the false prophets of Jeremiah 23 were doing), and so empty the churches (for who wants the church if we don't need the Saviour?).

Thirdly, Satan questions the goodness of God: 'God knows that when you eat of it your eyes will be opened, and you will be like God . . . ', just as today we're told that it's childish to be innocent, and that we'll be mature and enlightened if we just 'experiment a little' and 'discover a bit about the world'. We want to make our own decisions about what is right and wrong for us and 'be true to ourselves' and become devoted in worship to our own image. God is made out to be a cosmic 'spoilsport', making laws that hold us back. Satan is alive and well, spinning such lies through the media and the education system, and our evil hearts love to hear them. Indeed, we sometimes blame Satan for our sin when it is often our own desires that tempt us and we delight to hear Satan's invitations to sin. In the Lord's Prayer we ask, 'Help us not to be taken in by these ancient temptations.'

It is right to pray to be spared from temptation to sin. Not because God would tempt us, but because we want our Father to lead us in paths that avoid the places where our own desires tempt us to sin, or where Satan is likely to assault us with lies. We know that the Lord may allow us to be tempted by Satan, even if he himself is not the one doing the tempting, because Jesus was himself tempted shortly before teaching the Lord's Prayer. We read that, at the beginning of his public ministry as our representative, he resisted Satan's temptations by remaining loyal to the Word of God, as Adam had failed to do in the garden of Eden and as Israel failed to do in the desert:

> Then Jesus was led by the Spirit into the desert to be tempted by the devil. After fasting for forty days and forty nights, he was hungry. The tempter came to him and said, 'If you are the Son of God, tell these stones to become bread.' Jesus answered, 'It is written: "Man does not live by bread alone, but on every word that comes from the mouth of God."'
> (Matthew 4:1–4)

God the Holy Spirit led Jesus into the desert to be tempted, but the Spirit didn't induce Jesus to sin. We can see that it is not sinful to be tempted. It is sinful to give in to temptation. But we should beware of being over-confident and putting ourselves in situations where temptation is likely.

A helpful story is told of an Australian billionaire who was seeking a helmsman for his magnificent yacht. He advertised this prestigious and lucrative role all over the world, and three of the finest yachtsmen on the planet gathered in Sydney Harbour to demonstrate their skills to the owner. The first revealed his dazzling skills as he steered the multi-million-dollar boat within just a few yards of the harbour rocks at breathtaking speed. Everyone was impressed.

The second helmsman was even more remarkable. He steered the beautiful craft within inches of the cliffs at top speed with all the sails up, and everyone was nervously thrilled. He was incredible.

What could the last applicant do? Calmly, the final helmsman steered the luxury vessel out into the middle of the harbour and all aboard enjoyed a leisurely sail in the calm open water. The billionaire chose the last helmsman, explaining, 'You are all incredibly skilful, but I don't want a helmsman who takes risks with my boat. I would rather employ someone who enjoys the calm safety of steering clear of potential disaster.'

In the same way, Jesus wants us to steer clear of temptations. We are precious to him and he doesn't want us to push every boundary, playing with immorality and just getting away with it until, one day, we make a dreadful mistake and are smashed up on the rocks of sin. For example, many people would never have committed adultery if they had only steered clear of that particular colleague or that alcohol-fuelled social event. Jesus teaches us to pray for the Father's help to steer clear of the 'rocks'.

We have this assurance and warning from Paul, reflecting on the failures of Israel: 'If you think you are standing firm, be careful that you don't fall! No temptation has seized you except what is common to man. And God is faithful; he will not let you be tempted beyond what you can bear. But when you are tempted, he will also provide a way out so that you can stand up under it' (1 Corinthians 10:12–13). This is an encouragement that

God will always give us a way of escaping from temptation without yielding to it, but also a sober warning: we can never claim that we couldn't help it. God ensures that we can always resist temptation. If we fall, it is our fault and not Satan's, God's or anyone else's. In the Lord's Prayer we ask our Father to lead us in ways that, as far as possible, don't put us in situations where we will be tempted. This is a healthy awareness of our own weakness.

Jesus would later despair that his disciples were so careless that they couldn't see their need to engage in prayerful struggle to overcome temptation. On the night he was betrayed, when Jesus had led his disciples to the garden of Gethsemane to agonize in prayer about his impending ordeal, we read, 'Then he returned to his disciples and found them sleeping. "Could you men not keep watch with me for one hour?" he asked Peter. "Watch and pray so that you will not fall into temptation. The spirit is willing but the body is weak"' (Matthew 26:40–41). It was unclear what Jesus meant until the guards arrived with Judas to arrest him. The disciples were all for fighting, but Jesus rebuked Peter, saying, 'But how then would the Scriptures be fulfilled that say it must happen in this way?' (Matthew 26:54). Christ's agonized praying had brought him into full submission to the Father's will, published in Scripture, that he must be unjustly killed. The disciples, who had slept instead of praying, were unable to resist their own instincts to fight the need for the cross. They had not kept watch with Jesus against the temptations of Satan to disobey Scripture and avoid the cross, launched against him in the desert and finally repelled in the garden.

Our Father will lead us

When we pray 'Lead us not into temptation', we are not implying that our Father would lead us into sin. The meaning is 'Lead us in the way that is not temptation', i.e. a request for leading in paths of righteousness. We know that our Father leads both by his Word in Scripture (his revealed will) and by his sovereign shaping of circumstances (his secret will). So this prayer asks our Father to keep speaking through his Word as we read and hear it preached. And it is a commitment on our part not to harden our hearts to the contemporary voice of the Spirit speaking through the Scriptures, as Israel did in the desert (Hebrews 3:7).

We are, secondly, accepting that God is leading us by ordering the situations in which we find ourselves, and renewing our commitment to resist the temptations we face from Satan and our own desires. Such praying can help us to prepare ourselves: for example, if we are prone to react angrily to someone we find irritating, praying for help not to surrender to this temptation will be the ideal opportunity to plan how we might exit the situation to calm down before we finally 'lose it' once more!

Having asked for protection from temptation, the second great danger from which we need our heavenly Father's protection is Satan himself.

Protection from the evil one

Although the word used by Jesus for 'evil one' could mean evil in general or the evil one in particular, the grammar of the sentence means that he must be referring to Satan himself. Jesus was quite plain about the existence, malevolence and cunning of this vicious enemy of God and his people. 'Satan' means 'adversary', because he is opposed to God and his people. The New Testament warns clearly about his activity both in the hearts of unbelievers and in opposing the faith of believers.

Satan is at work in unbelievers. Jesus called him 'the prince of this world' and Paul calls him 'the ruler of the kingdom of the air, the spirit who is now at work in those who are disobedient' (John 14:30; Ephesians 2:2). Clearly, before we became Christians the devil was in all of us, promoting our disobedience to God and his Word. Jesus spoke of Satan as being like an ugly crow pecking at seed sown in a farmer's field, as he snatches away the gospel word from people's minds before it sinks in (Mark 4:15). He also spoke of Satan as being like 'a strong man' who holds unbelievers bound (Mark 3:27). Jesus came to overcome him and release his captives and 'destroy the devil's work' in this world by his death and resurrection (1 John 3:8). We read a powerful demonstration of this liberation in the expulsion of a legion of demons from the poor Gerasene demoniac (Mark 5:1–20). This man did not just have a psychiatric illness. He was displaying the debilitating effects of sin (promoted by Satan in all our lives), extreme in him because of the multiple demons possessing him, for us to witness Jesus' total mastery of Satan. The demoniac was antisocial, living outside the village in the tombs, violent and beyond control. He was distressed and self-harming, crying out night and day with no rest. But Jesus delivered him from his violence and anguish, with absolute authority over the demonic servants of Satan. Jesus threw them into some pigs, as one day he will throw them into the fires of hell. And the man was restored, dressed for social reintegration, in his right mind for thinking straight, and calmly at peace with God and man through Christ. No wonder he wanted to go with Jesus. But, like us, he had to stay and tell the village what Jesus had done for him. Such deliverance is known to all Christians when we become Christians. When we pray 'Deliver us from evil', we are asking God to continue protecting us from this activity of Satan in our lives.

The New Testament teaches that Christians continually face the attacks of Satan from three particular directions:

Disunity in churches

Division within Christian congregations (which is different from the healthy diversity of congregations and denominations necessary to reach different regions and cultures) undermines God's plan to unite all things under Christ. Paul urges his readers to resist Satan's schemes to disunite congregations with a famous passage about spiritual warfare:

> Finally, be strong in the Lord . . . For our struggle is not against flesh and blood, but against . . . the spiritual forces of evil in the heavenly realms. Stand firm then, with the belt of truth . . . the breastplate of righteousness . . . and . . . your feet fitted with the readiness that comes from the gospel of peace . . . take up the shield of faith . . . the helmet of salvation and the sword of the Spirit which is the word of God. And pray in the Spirit . . .
> (Ephesians 6:10–18)

This passage reveals that our enemies are evil spiritual forces, that our task is to stand firm in unity in Christ, and that our protection is in the convictions of the gospel. All the pieces of armour (coming from Old Testament descriptions of God) are the truths of the gospel, defended by the sword of the Spirit, which is the Word of God, and by prayer in the Holy Spirit. This battle for unity in the churches is constant and we must 'not give the devil a foothold' (Ephesians 4:27). A second source of spiritual attack is through suffering.

Suffering in Christians

The apostle urges us:

> Humble yourselves, therefore, under God's mighty hand, that he may lift you up in due time. Cast all your anxiety on him because he cares for you. Be self-controlled and alert. Your enemy the devil prowls around like a roaring lion looking for someone to devour. Resist him, standing firm in the faith, because you know

that your brothers throughout the world are undergoing the
same kind of sufferings.
(1 Peter 5:6–9)

The way that the devil is to be resisted reveals a great deal. We
resist him by standing firm in our faith in God. Christians don't
need exorcisms or incantations and spells: we need to remain
confident in God. This shows that Satan's intention is to get us
to abandon our faith in God. The fact that he is defeated simply
by our standing firm in faith reveals that his only power is to
question our faith. Satan may be as ferocious and dangerous as
a roaring lion, but we are reassured that he is on Jesus' leash. We
are told, 'Resist the devil and he will flee from you' (James 4:7).

Satan does not control any aspect of the life of a Christian –
we belong to our Father, and he is sovereign. There is no struggle
between God and the devil, for our Father is utterly sovereign
and Christ has disarmed the rebel and will soon crush the serpent
under his feet. The only thing Satan can do to God's people is to
question our faith and promote doubt in our Father. He uses our
sufferings as the opportunity to challenge God's love and care
for us, so the way to resist him is to recognize that our fellow
Christians throughout the world are suffering the same kind
of troubles. Satan loves to suggest that God doesn't care about
us, or that we are uniquely troubled because we have been
abandoned. It's that lie from the garden again about God
wanting to spoil our lives. The background to Satan using our
suffering to make us question God is given in the magisterial
treatment of the matter in the book of Job.

When the Lord showed Satan that Job was a man who was
'blameless and upright, a man who fears God and shuns evil'
(1:8), Satan claimed that this was only because Job was blessed
by God and that Job would abandon the Lord if his life involved
suffering. So Satan was given permission by the Lord to afflict
Job to test his faith in God, and to glorify God in the heavenly
realms by maintaining faith even when life was utterly miserable

and troubles were coming thick and fast. Job was never told that this was why he faced such dreadful loss and hardship. But we, the readers, are told, so that we can learn that we also may be afflicted for a while by Satan in order for our faith to be tested. But, in the end, we shall, like Job, be greatly rewarded by God if we can remain faithful. So let us hear Peter's challenge and, inspired by the examples of Job and Jesus, who never abandoned their faith in God's goodness, resist the devil's temptations to sinful resentment against our Father.

The lies of false teaching

The third direction from which Satan may afflict believers is in deceptive false teaching. The 'father of lies' will do all he can to undermine our Father of truth. Paul writes, 'Satan himself masquerades as an angel of light' (2 Corinthians 11:14) and 'the Spirit clearly says that in later times some will abandon the faith and follow deceiving spirits and things taught by demons.' Who could teach such things? Paul continues, 'Such teachings come through hypocritical liars.' What sort of dreadful falsehood could this devilish teaching be? Paul explains, 'They forbid people to marry and order them to abstain from certain foods . . . For every-thing God created is good, and nothing is to be rejected if it is received with thanksgiving, because it is consecrated by the word of God and prayer' (1 Timothy 4:1–5). The devil's lies are heard in religion, even religion that uses biblical words, forbidding what God allows and making our loving Creator and Father seem cruel. When religious people impose vows of chastity or fasting or forbid the godly enjoyment of entertainment or alcohol, they may mean well, but they are peddling the lies of demons! Our Creator intends us to enjoy his goodness, within the constraints of his Word (which is no more restrictive than a fish tank is restrictive of a goldfish), and with prayerful gratitude to God (which is the opposite of the complaining pagan). Religion rules through fear of punishment or the reward of pride, but it produces hypocrites because it cannot soften the heart with the grace of the gospel. Only an understanding and delight in God's grace can produce real godliness in us because it generates the desire to please God and to shape our lives to be loving like God.

The devil assaults us through disunity in our churches, through doubts in our suffering and through the lies of religion. We can resist him by clinging to the gospel of God in faith.

In the Lord's Prayer, we ask our Father for strength to survive both the testing of our faith in order that it might be purified, and the questioning of our faith by Satan, that we might retain our confidence in God.

Deliverance

In leading us in the way that does not go through trials and temptations, our Father is 'delivering' us from evil. This can mean both delivering us from getting into such situations (i.e. never facing them) and getting us out of these situations (i.e. escaping from them).

In both cases of 'deliverance', our Father will be exercising a power over the devil that was demonstrated and secured for ever at the cross of Christ. At the very point at which Satan seemed to be victorious, when Jesus was nailed to a cross, accused by Satan of all our sins, the power of Satan was decisively broken. As a result, 'the God of peace will soon crush Satan under your feet' and Jesus will throw him into the 'eternal fire' prepared for him and his angels (Romans 16:20; Matthew 25:41).

It is vital to understand that the devil is not powerful because he is powerful enough to compete with God. Indeed, since God is utterly sovereign, the devil has no power of his own. The battle between God and Satan is more one-sided than the tug of war between a fisherman and the maggot on the end of his line! The only power that the devil has over us is our sin and guilt.

The devil tries to appeal to God's own law to accuse us of sin, in order to condemn us to the punishment that we deserve (eternal death in hell), and so to frustrate God's great plan to provide a people to praise his Son. He is the 'accuser' of God's people who is pictured accusing Joshua the High Priest when the Lord says, '"The LORD rebuke you, Satan! . . . Is not this man a burning stick snatched from the fire?" Now Joshua was dressed in filthy clothes . . . The angel said . . . "Take off his filthy clothes. See, I have taken away your sin and I will put rich garments on you"' (Zechariah 3:2–4). Satan's power of accusation is defeated by the forgiveness of our sin (because our sin was punished in Christ at the cross) and the provision of the righteousness we need in Christ (because Christ was obedient even unto death on a cross).

When Paul writes, 'And having disarmed the powers and authorities, he made a public spectacle of them, triumphing over them by the cross' (Colossians 2:15), he has just explained how God did this. 'He forgave us all our sins, having cancelled the written code, with its regulations, that was against us and that stood opposed to us . . . nailing it to the cross' (2:13–14). The charge that we must be punished in accordance with God's law has been met because in Christ we have been punished. We are no longer guilty, so Satan has been 'disarmed'!

Again we read in Hebrews, 'Since the children have flesh and blood, he [Christ] too shared in their humanity so that by his death he might destroy him who holds the power of death – that is, the devil – and free those who all their lives were held in slavery by their fear of death' (Hebrews 2:14–15). Death is God's just judgment on our sin. The reason that Satan is said to 'hold the power of death' is that he is the 'accuser' who seeks our death according to God's law, and not that he himself is in power. But since Christ became man and died our death for us, the sentence is exhausted in him and we are free from accusation and death. This is why Jesus says of his death, 'Now is the time for judgment on this world; now the prince of this world will be driven out' (John 12:31), and why Christians are said to triumph over Satan 'by the blood of the Lamb' (Revelation 12:11).

We are now, therefore, gloriously free from Satan's rule and power. Our Father 'has rescued us from the dominion of darkness and brought us into the kingdom of the Son he loves, in whom we have redemption, the forgiveness of sins' (Colossians 1:13–14)

This means that Christians can never be demon-possessed or retaken by Satan from Christ. I don't question that many who become Christians, especially when they have been involved in occult practice and Satanism, must be delivered of their demons by God as they come to believe the gospel of Christ. I don't even question that they may become Christians over a period of time, as their faith in Christ clarifies and demons are finally expelled by the Holy Spirit. I do question that a person who has been saved and transferred from the kingdom of Satan into the kingdom of God and indwelt by the Holy Spirit of God can ever be possessed by demons again (even though the sins of a Christian still serve the devil's evil purposes). Jesus proved the incompatibility of the two kingdoms when he said to those who wondered if he cast out demons by the power of the devil, 'If I drive out demons by the finger of God, then the kingdom of God has come to you' (Luke 11:20). Jesus is saying that demons can be cast out only by the power of God and, if they are cast out, then the kingdom of God is present. Jesus assumes that one could not have both – you could not have demons and the kingdom of God present at the same time in the same person because they are mutually exclusive. This is proof that Christians cannot be demon-possessed; they are either not Christians or not demon-possessed.

The wonderful news of the gospel is that Christ has conquered Satan and delivered us from his powers. When we pray 'Deliver us from evil', we ask our Father to continue protecting us from our defeated and doomed enemy, the devil.

In the Lord's Prayer, we ask our Father to protect us from trials of painful testing and temptations to sin, and to apply the victory of the cross to the evil one and keep us delivered from him.

In this sixth petition of the Lord's Prayer, Jesus is
teaching us to enjoy God as

VICTORIOUS DELIVERER
. . . AS ENDANGERED TRAVELLERS

So how might we pray this in practice?

As she lay in bed trying to read the latest Hosseini novel
by lamplight, Caz drifted into reviewing a most amazing
day and reflected on her experience of praying the Lord's
Prayer. She had never expected it to have the impact that
it had had: she'd started praying in the tube, confronted
a colleague at work about blasphemy, advised a church
friend about her unconverted flatmates, prayed with a
man who might ask her to marry him (including a prayer
about going to Vietnam as a missionary), talked to one
of her best non-Christian friends about being forgiven,
and all in less than twenty-four hours. The Father was
clearly showing her how involved in her life he really
was. Given all this, she could hardly neglect the chance
to finish the Lord's Prayer. She put aside the book and
closed her eyes to pray.
  *'And lead us not into temptation, but deliver us from
evil.'*
  'I do praise you, Father, that you are constantly
protecting us from dangers we never even know about
and that your Spirit constantly leads us through life by
guiding us through your Word and arranging the
circumstances of our lives. Father, thank you that you
never forget or lose us . . . er . . .

'Please don't lead me into testing that I can't cope with, Father. I suppose I do need to learn how to endure through hardship, but please don't let me fall apart, Father, and . . . er . . .

'Please don't let me be tempted to sin by Satan or my own desires without being able to resist it. Please help me and Guy not to get carried away, Father, and also help me to be ready to give up my comforts and my career to go to Vietnam if you want me to and . . . er . . .

'Please also deliver us from evil. Father, thank you that Satan was defeated on the cross and that all his accusations against me and all my brothers and sisters in your family have been answered by Jesus there. Thank you so much that I don't need to be superstitious or frightened of demons or Satan . . . and . . .

'Please deliver me and our church from the evil of disunity and division, Father, and please deliver us from doubting you when we face suffering. Father, help me to resist the devil, remembering that all over the world your people are suffering and remaining loyal to you (and please help the Christians in North Korea and Saudi Arabia and Pakistan and China, Father. Please give them hope in you) and please also deliver me and our church from false teaching . . . so please help Pastor Jack and all the staff team to teach us sound doctrine and to refute errors, Father, and then . . . '

The book fell off the bed and Caz was finally engulfed by sleep, safe in her heavenly Father's arms.

And then at 6am her mobile began to ring . . .

And meanwhile . . .

The phone was ringing but Caz wasn't answering. It was only 6am but Peter hoped that she had her mobile switched on. Apparently Mike had tried from Australia but without success. As the oldest brother, however, Peter felt some responsibility for telling the whole family.

'Hello?' Caz's voice was bleary with sleep. 'Who is it?'

'Caz, it's Peter. Are you alright?'

'Yes, well no. Why are you ringing at this unearthly hour – what's wrong?'

'I'm sorry, Caz, but I thought you'd want to know as soon as possible. It's Grandpa Harold. Bad news, I'm afraid. He's had a massive heart attack.'

'Oh no!' cried Caz weakly, sensing there was more. She and her Granddad had always had a very special relationship. 'Is he going to be OK?'

'No, I'm sorry, Caz, he died in his bed before the ambulance even got here, and Dad found him this morning. I'm ringing from Mum and Dad's actually.' Peter was trying to stay strong, but his voice was faltering now.

'Oh,' said Caz, not knowing what to say. She couldn't take it in – too much like one of her weird dreams. 'How's Mum? Have you told everyone else? What about Tony? And Mike and Sarah are in Australia!'

'I think Mum's in shock really. She's sort of dazed and weepy but not distraught. Dad's with her. And everyone else knows now – I rang Tony. They're four and a half hours ahead in Afghanistan and the base commander got him on the phone for me. Apparently he can probably get home within a week. And Mike and Sarah and Milly were flying back from Oz tomorrow anyway, so they'll be back at the weekend.'

'Oh', said Caz, suddenly engulfed by sadness. She began sobbing.

'Listen, Caz, I was thinking, why don't you come straight down to us on the train. You can ring work when you get here – or would you like one of us to come and get you? Bring enough to stay a few days. Stay as long as you like.'

'When will the funeral be? Can we see his body?' Caz was confused.

'Yes, apparently we can, tomorrow or Monday, I think. I'll check with the funeral directors tomorrow. The funeral doesn't have to be for at least a week. I'll have to check that Pastor Jack's free. I haven't rung him yet. I'm sure he will be. After all, we've all known him ever since he arrived here in Maidstone.'

'OK,' said Caz. She thought for a moment and then accepted Peter's suggestion. 'I'll pack some clothes and come down this morning. I think I would like to stay with you and Mum and Dad if that's possible. Thanks, Peter.'

'That's no problem – just call me on your mobile any time.'

'He's with Jesus now, isn't he, having a good time?' asked Caz.

'Yes, and with Grandma too. He'll be so happy to see the Father. Do you know, Mum says that he's prayed the Lord's Prayer every day since he became a Christian fifty-eight years ago? That's why Mum uses it so much. So I think he'll feel like he's home now.'

Caz was still stunned. 'Bet he does. Thanks for calling, Peter, see you later.'

Caz sat upright in bed for a few moments, unable to move. And then she cried . . . and cried . . . and cried. After a shower, she came back and knelt by her bed. She prayed the Lord's Prayer from beginning to end, as her grandfather had apparently done all his life. She would do the same. She was looking forward to being with the Father already. *'For yours is the kingdom, the power and the glory, for ever and ever. Amen.'* And after that, she phoned Guy.

9 'The kingdom, the power and the glory . . .'

(A fitting conclusion)

Most people are used to ending the Lord's Prayer with some version of the words 'For yours is the kingdom, the power and the glory, for ever and ever, Amen'. There has been considerable debate about whether these words actually come from Jesus. They do not appear in the very earliest translations that we have, but they are certainly consistent with biblical teaching. They provide a wonderfully fitting conclusion to this glorious prayer, and they have been used widely in every generation of Christian worship. Even though they are probably not from the lips of Jesus, they do remind us of three marvellous attributes of God that are the reason why we pray the Lord's Prayer.

The word 'for' indicates that what follows is the reason that we pray the Lord's Prayer and why we believe our Father will answer us. We might worry that it is rude to reason and argue with God. Far from it! The Bible is full of examples of believers being approved for pleading and reasoning with God, humbly but fervently. As Job says, 'I would state my case before him and fill my mouth with arguments' (Job 23:4).

As human fathers want their children to reveal the reasons and feelings behind their requests, so that their kids can know that their fathers understand them when deciding how to respond, so our Father in heaven wants us to open our hearts and reveal our motives to him. The hymn-writer Isaac Watts helpfully identified seven biblical grounds for pleading with God:

- from the desperation of our need;
- from the perfections of God's wise and powerful nature;
- from the relationship that God has established with us as our Creator, King and Father;
- from the promises he has made in Scripture;
- from the honour and reputation of God;
- from the great things that God has done before; and
- from our new status in Christ.

We are now entitled (in Christ) to plead as needy children with our loving Father. All these ways of pleading honour him. As Jacob was approved by God for wrestling all night with God for his blessing (Genesis 32), so our Father wants us to pour our energies into our relationship with him, wrestling in prayer with him for his blessing rather than seeking it from the world around us.

The little word 'yours' is also important. It reminds us that these glorious attributes are God's and not ours. This is particularly important, because we are proudly self-reliant and because the last three petitions have been concerned with our own needs. This conclusion is a simple but climactic 'doxology', an expression of praise to God that brings us back to our Father to find our deepest satisfaction in honouring him. We end the prayer with this humbling reminder of our own lowliness, weakness and shame and that our Father is great (yours is the kingdom), strong (yours is the power) and wonderful (yours is the glory). This is the right attitude in which to finish praying and go out to worship him with our whole life.

Even the tiny word 'is' contains a precious truth. While our hopes for the future await the return of Christ with the kingdom of God, when all the petitions of the Lord's Prayer will be perfectly accomplished, we are reminded that our Father is as sovereign, almighty and magnificent today as he will be then. Our Father is in total control of our world and our lives right now.

The particular grounds for praying all six petitions of the Lord's Prayer are three related aspects of his being: his kingship, his power and his glory.

Yours is 'the kingdom'

Our Father is the sovereign King of kings who has enthroned our Lord Jesus Christ as King over the growing and coming kingdom of God. Everything is his and one day everyone will bow before him and acknowledge it.

This truth purifies our ambitions. With these words, we pledge ourselves to work not for the extension of our own little kingdoms, but for the advancement of his kingdom (in evangelism) as citizens of his kingdom (in holiness) in hope of his kingdom (for the glory of the King).

We need this reminder that our ambitions for our own kingdoms, whether in a business, a sport, a family or a church ministry, will all come to nothing if they are for our own glory. A fabulous little poem by Shelley, *Ozymandias*, exposes the futile ambitions of man. It begins, 'I met a traveller from an antique land', who tells of an extraordinary little crumbled statue of a once-great emperor, which stands in the middle of the desert. All around the statue, his empire is buried under the sands of time. The poem ends:

And on the pedestal these words appear:
'My name is Ozymandias, king of kings:
Look on my works, ye Mighty, and despair!'
Nothing beside remains. Round the decay
Of that colossal wreck, boundless and bare,
The lone and level sands stretch far away'.[1]

This sobering truth that human kingdoms will not survive into eternity is being recalled when we pray 'Your kingdom come'.

God alone is King. Psalm 145 calls us to praise this King (1–2) because he is great (3–7), gracious (8–13), faithful (14–16) and righteous (17–20). It concludes 'Let every creature praise his holy name for ever and ever.' Our Father is the sovereign King and under his rule we will flourish for ever.

Yours is 'the power'

Our Father is Almighty God. He has the power to do precisely as he pleases and is subject to no-one and nothing. Wonderfully, he therefore has the power to answer the petitions of the Lord's Prayer, and all our prayers, in exactly the best way for accomplishing his eternal purposes and the good of his people.

This truth purifies our confidence. With these words we pledge ourselves to work, not in reliance upon our own strength but upon his. We will certainly need the power of his Holy Spirit to hallow his reputation, extend his kingdom, obey his will, find daily bread, forgive others as we are forgiven, and avoid temptation and evil, and to keep on doing this day after day, month after month and year after year. We know that as we 'continue to work out our salvation with fear and trembling', we can do so only because 'it is God who works in you to will and to act according to his good purpose' (Philippians 2:12–13). We recognize our utter dependence on our Father with these simple words.

Psalm 139 calls us to submit to our Father's transformation because he is all-knowing (omniscient): 'You know everything about me' (1–6), ever-present (omnipresent): 'You are always with me' (7–12) and all-powerful (omnipotent): 'You made every part of me' (13–18). The Psalmist calls us to surrender before God Almighty with the words, 'Search me, O God, and know my heart; test me and know my anxious thoughts. See if there is any offensive way in me and lead me in the way everlasting.'

I recall talking outside the Dome of the Rock in Jerusalem to a Palestinian Christian friend of mine who had been born again from a Muslim background. I asked if he was frightened of being killed for converting to Christianity. He replied with simple and humbling faith, 'Our heavenly Father is in control and my life is safe in his hands. I am content to trust him.'

When we pray, we need to remember that our Father is Almighty God and in his powerful hands we are safe for ever.

Yours is 'the glory'

When Moses asked God, 'Show me your glory' [lit., weightiness], the Lord revealed his name or character, 'The LORD, the LORD, the compassionate and gracious God, slow to anger, abounding in love and faithfulness, maintaining love to thousands, and forgiving wickedness, rebellion and sin. Yet he does not leave the guilty unpunished . . . ' (Exodus 34:6–7). Our Father's glory is revealed in his character, especially in being merciful and just. This glory became incarnate in Jesus, of whom we read, 'The Son is the radiance of God's glory and the exact representation of his being' (Hebrews 1:3), and the apostle John recalls with breathless excitement, 'We have seen his glory, the glory of the One and Only . . . full of grace and truth' (John 1:14). This glory of God's merciful and just character was most fully revealed at the cross. And it will be evident to all when Christ returns, when 'men will see the Son of Man coming in clouds with great power and glory' (Mark 13:26).

This truth purifies our pride. With these words we pledge ourselves to live, work and pray, at home, at work, at church and at play, to enhance the glory and reputation of God rather than ourselves.

Psalm 103 calls us to praise the Lord and not forget all his benefits. As our heavenly Father has showered upon us the blessings of his grace, we are urged to recall that, he is our loving

Saviour (2–5), he is our merciful Redeemer (6–12) and he is our everlasting Father (13–18). The Psalmist begins and ends the psalm by rousing his own hard heart and ours to glorify our glorious heavenly Dad with the words, 'Praise the LORD, O my soul'.

One of the finest examples of living for the glory of God is the colourful life of Sir Henry Havelock, the respected English general and hero of the siege of Lucknow in India. A grateful nation honoured him with a statue in Trafalgar Square in London. Whatever we now think of the British presence in India, Havelock distinguished himself as a Christian soldier, living for the glory of God rather than for his own advancement. He pioneered the distribution of Bibles and the organization of Bible studies for all ranks, established new discipline among his soldiers that kept them from prostitutes and alcohol, and won the respect of the nation for his faith in Christ. Whatever our role in life, we can all seek to live in godliness for the advancement of the glory of our Father rather than our own reputation. When we pray 'and the glory', we are committing ourselves to this priority in our life.

Conclusion

As we conclude our look at the spectacularly wonderful Lord's Prayer, the words 'for yours is the kingdom, the power and the glory' are beautifully expounded for us in the marvellous prayer of David when he rejoiced in the commitment of God's people to the building of a temple for God under Solomon's direction. This is a fitting parallel for Christians ending the Lord's Prayer and committing ourselves to work together towards all that we've asked for in the Prayer, for our heavenly Father's glory alone:

> Praise be to you, O LORD,
>> God of our father Israel,
>> from everlasting to everlasting.

Yours, O LORD, is the greatness and the power
   and the glory and the majesty and the splendour,
   for everything in heaven and earth is yours.
Yours, O LORD, is the kingdom;
   you are exalted as head over all.
Wealth and honour come from you;
   you are the ruler of all things.
In your hands are strength and power
   to exalt and give strength to all.
Now, our God, we give you thanks,
   and praise your glorious name.
(1 Chronicles 29:10–13)

Amen!

Appendix –
What is prayer . . . and why should we pray?

What is prayer?

Prayer means speaking to God. It is our side of the personal conversation that lies at the heart of a Christian's relationship with God. God speaks to us through the words of Scripture and we respond to him in words of prayer.

In his classic little book *Praying in the Spirit*, written from Bedford Gaol where he was imprisoned, John Bunyan (author of *A Pilgrim's Progress*) brilliantly defined prayer as:

> a sincere, sensible, affectionate pouring out of the heart or soul to God, through Christ, in the strength and assistance of the Spirit, for such things as God has promised, or according to his Word, for the good of the church, with submission in faith to the will of God.[1]

Bunyan provides important principles for ensuring that our prayer is genuine and not just empty waffle that our heavenly Father ignores.

Real prayer is 'sincere' (i.e. honest and genuine), for otherwise 'when you ask, you do not receive, because you ask with wrong motives' (James 4:3).

Real prayer is 'sensible' (i.e. fervent and passionate), because 'you will seek me and find me when you seek me with all your heart' (Jeremiah 29:13).

Real prayer is 'affectionate' (i.e. confident in God's goodness), for 'he who doubts is like a wave of the sea, blown and tossed by the wind. That man should not think he will receive anything from the Lord' (James 1:6–7).

Real prayer is 'through Christ in the strength and assistance of the Spirit' (i.e. empowered and conveyed to the Father by the Holy Spirit), for 'the Spirit himself intercedes for us with groans that words cannot express' (Romans 8:26).

Real prayer is 'for such things as God has promised' (i.e. claiming what God has offered in his Word), for 'this is the confidence we have in approaching God: that if we ask anything according to his will, he hears us' (1 John 5:14).

Real prayer is 'for the good of the church' (i.e. not selfish but for all God's people), for we must 'keep on praying for all the saints' (Ephesians 6:18).

Real prayer is 'with submission in faith to the will of God' (i.e. surrendering to God's will rather than asserting our own), for 'how much more will your Father in heaven give good gifts to those who ask him!' (Matthew 7:11).

By contrast, fake prayer that insults our Father and receives nothing is dishonest (mindless or proud), passionless (apathetic or careless), doubtful (sceptical or cynical), superficial (disengaged or repetitive), unspiritual (unbiblical or unconverted), selfish (loveless or self-indulgent) or demanding (proud or manipulative).

Why should we pray?

If prayer is not about getting God to submit to our wills but about submitting ourselves to his will, the obvious question is, why do we bother? If God 'does not lie or change his mind' (1 Samuel 15:29), and if he 'knows what you need before you ask him' (Matthew 6:8), then what is the point of praying at all?

In his masterly chapter on prayer in his famous *Institutes*, the great Reformer John Calvin clarified six reasons for praying:

a) **Dependence** – so that our hearts become inflamed with a 'burning desire to seek, love and serve him . . . and become accustomed in every need to flee to him as to a sacred anchor'; in other words, learning to depend upon him;

b) **Purity** – so that our hearts don't nurture desires and longings of which 'we should be ashamed to make him a witness'; in other words, purifying the desires of our hearts;

c) **Gratitude** – so that we learn to 'receive his benefits with true gratitude', which means learning contentment with what our Father provides;

d) **Appreciation** – so that we 'meditate upon his kindness more ardently', leading us to appreciate more deeply his generosity and faithfulness;

e) **Enjoyment** – so that we may 'embrace with greater delight' the things we receive from praying, namely to enjoy without inhibition the many good gifts that God provides for our happiness;

f) **Trust** – so that we learn to 'confirm his providence', which means we learn to trust God to provide our daily needs and never to let us down.

Calvin summarized such prayer as 'digging up the treasures' that are promised in Scripture. Certainly, it is our experience that God delays giving us the things he plans to grant until we ask for them in prayer. Though God had always planned to give them, from our perspective things change when we pray, and so he encourages us to talk to him by withholding gifts *until* we pray – in other words, things happen when we pray!

As a loving human parent will withhold gifts from a toddler until he asks properly in order to teach humble dependence on those who care for him, so God teaches us to pray in dependence, purity, gratitude, appreciation, enjoyment and trust, by withholding blessings until we learn to talk to him properly.

A godly archbishop of Canterbury was once asked by a sceptical journalist if answers to prayer were simply coincidences. He wisely replied, 'I don't know – but when I stop praying the coincidences seem to stop happening too!'

Now to him who is able to do immeasurably more than all we ask or imagine, according to his power that is at work within us, to him be glory in the church and in Christ Jesus throughout all generations, for ever and ever! Amen.

(Ephesians 3:20–21)

Notes

Chapter 1

1. J. C. Ryle, *Practical Religion*, (Darlington: Evangelical Press, 2002), p. 73.
2. *Praying* by J. I. Packer and Carolyn Nystrom (IVP, 2006) is hugely helpful. Hallesby's *Prayer* (IVP, 1948), Baughen's *The Prayer Principle* (Christian Focus, 2007), Dunn's *Don't Just Stand There . . . Pray Something* (Zondervan, 2001), Carson's outstanding *A Call to Spiritual Reformation* (IVP, 1992), Calvin's *Institutes* (Westminster/John Knox Press, US, 2001), Thomas's *Praying the Saviour's Way* (Christian Focus, 2009), Johnson's excellent *When Grace Comes Alive* (Christian Focus, 2003), Huffman's *Forgive Us Our Prayers* (Christian Focus, 2005) and Derek Prime's outstanding *The Lord's Prayer for Today* (Day One, 1996) are also all great.
3. Luke 9:18, 28; 11:1; 23:34, 46.
4. John 11:41; 12:27; 17:1–26.
5. Luke 10:21; John 17:1, 24; Matthew 26:42, 26; Luke 23:34; John 17:15.

Chapter 2

1. J. I. Packer, *Knowing God* (London: Hodder & Stoughton, 1993), p. 226.
2. Patrick Johnstone and Jason Mandryk, *Operation World* (Carlisle: Authentic Lifestyle, 2005).

Chapter 4

1. Rodney Stark, *The Rise of Christianity: A Sociologist Reconsiders History* (Princeton University Press, 1996).

Chapter 5

1. C. S. Lewis, *The Problem of Pain* (New York: Macmillan, 1940).
2. J. I. Packer and Carolyn Nystrom, *Praying* (Nottingham: IVP, 2006), p. 155.

Chapter 7

1. The Very Revd Jeffrey John, speaking in a BBC Radio 4 Lent talk, 4 April 2007.
2. Steve Chalke and Alan Mann, *The Lost Message of Jesus* (Grand Rapids, MI: Zondervan, 2003), pp. 182–183.

Chapter 8

1. Richard Dawkins, *The God Delusion* (London: Bantam Press, 2006).
2. Dan Brown, *The Da Vinci Code* (London: Corgi, 2004).

Chapter 9

1. *Ozymandias* was written in December 1817 during a writing contest between Shelley and his friend Horace Smith, and first published in Leigh Hunt's *Examiner* of 11 January 1818.

Appendix

1. John Bunyan, *Praying in the Spirit*, (UK: Meadow Books, 2007 [1662]).

Bibliography

The Lord's Prayer

G. Bray (2007), *Yours is the Kingdom*, Nottingham: IVP.

D. Carson, ed. (2002), *Teach Us to Pray*, Grand Rapids/Carlisle: Baker/Paternoster.

J. Huffman Jr (2005), *Forgive Us Our Prayers*, Fearn: Christian Focus.

T. L. Johnson (2003), *When Grace Comes Alive*, Fearn: Christian Focus.

P. Lewis (1995), *The Lord's Prayer*, London: Hodder & Stoughton.

D. Prime (1996), *The Lord's Prayer for Today*, Leominster: Day One.

P. Ryken (2002), *The Prayer of Our Lord*, Wheaton, IL: Crossway Books.

J. E. White (2005), *The Prayer God Longs For*, Leicester: IVP.

Prayer

J. Bunyan (1662), *Prayer*, Edinburgh: Banner of Truth Trust.

D. Carson, ed. (2002), *Teach Us to Pray*, Carlisle: Baker/Paternoster.

P. T. Forsyth (1916), *The Soul of Prayer*, Carlisle: Paternoster.

G. Goldsworthy (2003), *Prayer and the Knowledge of God*, Leicester: IVP.

O. Hallesby (1948), *Prayer*, Leicester: IVP.

J. I. Packer and C. Nystrom (2006), *Praying*, Nottingham: IVP.

General

J. Calvin (1960) (ed. McNeill, trans. Battles), *Institutes of the Christian Religion*, Philadelphia: Westminster.

D. Carson, ed. (1984), *The Expositor's Bible Commentary*, Vol. 8, Grand Rapids, MI: Zondervan.

J. Frame (2002), *The Doctrine of God*, Phillipsburg, NJ: P. & R. Publishing.

J. Frame (2006), *Salvation Belongs to the Lord*, Phillipsburg, NJ: P. & R. Publishing.

L. Morris (1992), *The Gospel According to Matthew*, Leicester: IVP.

J. I. Packer (1993), *Knowing God*, London: Hodder & Stoughton.

J. C. Ryle, (2002), *Practical Religion*, Darlington: Evangelical Press.

R. Stark (1996), *The Rise of Christianity*, Princeton, NJ: Princeton University Press.

www.ivpbooks.com

For more details of books published by IVP, visit our website where you will find all the latest information, including:

Book extracts	Downloads
Author interviews	Online bookshop
Reviews	Christian bookshop finder

You can also sign up for our regular email newsletters, which are tailored to your particular interests, and tell others what you think about this book by posting a review.

We publish a wide range of books on various subjects including:

Christian living	Small-group resources
Key reference works	Topical issues
Bible commentary series	Theological studies